INTERNAL CONTROLS
IN BANKING

INTERNAL CONTROLS IN BANKING

Edited by
RAY KINSELLA

JOHN WILEY & SONS

Chichester • New York • Brisbane • Toronto • Singapore

CONTENTS

About the Contributors

Steve Almond is Group Partner, Touche Ross.

Cyril Bennett is Senior Manager, Treasury Risk Control, AIB Group Treasury.

Ray Kinsella is Visiting Professor of Financial Services, Graduate School of Business, UCD, and Professor of Banking and Financial Services, University of Ulster at Coleraine.

Graham Leese is Manager, Standards & Techniques, National Westminster Bank.

John F. Mogg is Director-General EU Commission DG XV (Internal Market and Financial Services).

Brian Quinn is Executive Director and Head of Financial Supervision, Bank of England.

John Trethowan is Manager, Strategic Planning, Northern Bank Group.

Anthony Walsh is Dean, Dublin City University Business School.

FOREWORD

"The inspectors are in." These words have for decades struck fear into the hearts of even the most compliant bank managers and staff. What followed was a ritual dance of mutual distrust and, quite often, nit-picking on an heroic scale. Perhaps that style suited the command and control environment of what were simple banks — deposit-taking and lending were the core products, indeed very often the only products.

Today these same banks are financial service conglomerates, offering a wide range of services, some extremely complex and most increasingly regulated. At the same time, competition (and good business practice) means that within defined parameters more decisions are being taken closer to the customer, increasing the risk of fraud or error. Pay for performance has introduced yet another potentially incremental risk factor for financial institutions. Overall, an explosive cocktail for the financial institution of the 1990s.

Fortunately for the depositor, the science (or is it an art?) of internal controls has not stood still. This book is a welcome addition to the knowledge base of those wanting to understand how state of the art internal controls operate. The various essays deal with all aspects of internal control, from a variety of perspectives but always with authority. Underlying all of them is the enormous change of attitude that has taken place in relation to internal controls — the role of audit and compliance functions as partners in the business, not snoops or enemies; the recognition that what gives an organisation adequacy of internal control rests not on the rule book, but essentially on the culture where people know instinctively what is right, are encouraged to express concerns on matters of internal control or risk and, above all, where everyone understands that a problem is to be shared, not uncovered by an audit.

David Went
Chief Executive
Coutts Private Bank Ltd

For Ita

INTRODUCTION:
INTERNAL CONTROLS IN BANKING

Ray Kinsella

Professor of Banking and Financial Services, University of Ulster
at Coleraine and Visiting Professor of Financial Services,
Graduate School of Business, University College Dublin

INTRODUCTION

Internal controls are now a central feature of the operational
and management structures of banks. Internal controls have
been defined[1] in terms of "systems established in order to provide reasonable assurance of effective and efficient operations,
reliable financial information and reporting and compliance
with laws and regulations."

Their essential purpose is to safeguard the financial integrity of the institutions. The need to protect against fraud —
whether perpetrated from within the bank or outside — has
always been of particular relevance to banks. Their highly lev-
eraged nature — pivoted on processing information and money
— means that they are uniquely vulnerable. Where controls
are deficient fraud, and even failure, are seldom far behind.

There has, in recent years, been an increase in scale and
complexity of such controls, reflecting the growth and dispersion of risk in banking. Developments in information technology (IT) and the globalisation of financial markets, including,
in particular, the wholesale markets, which it has facilitated,
has increased the *potential* for systemic risk. Equally, however,
IT has also created new possibilities for *managing* risk, for enhancing systems through which payments and other data are
transmitted, and, more generally, for developing internal con-

---

[1] See Chapter 4, Section 2.

trol systems to identify, track and help control risk. What is altogether a recent phenomenon is that, rather than being an operational unit (often fairly basic), such controls are now a pervasive part of the whole internal architecture of banks.

This development has occurred rapidly — since the middle 1980s — as part of the development of a wider compliance system encompassing prudential supervision and consumer protection as well as standards and systems to ensure the veracity of financial information and, more recently, corporate governance. It reflects a response by the supervisory authorities and the banks themselves to public concern over bank crises — as well as heightened expectations on the part of all stakeholders in relation to the integrity and relevance of financial statements, accountability and, more generally, corporate governance. The compliance burden — statutory and voluntary — has increased very considerably. So, too, has the cost.

It is important to be clear on the reasons why — and the manner in which — structural change and innovation in financial markets has had a pervasive impact on accounting-based controls in individual banks and in banking markets. Folkerts-Landau and Steinherr argue that:

> The financial and accounting statements of intermediaries have become much less useful as a guide to the safety and soundness of an institution. It has become possible to alter rapidly the risk profile of a bank or securities house by transforming on- and off-balance sheet positions. Position data gathered at periodic intervals, say monthly or weekly, no longer provide an adequate picture of the actual risk or potential exposures. When bank business was mainly on-balance sheet, it was a much slower process to "bet the bank".[2]

The consequence of all this has been a concomitant responsibility on the part of bankers for the development of new control systems. The development of the derivatives markets is a case in point. Writing on this, the President of the Federal Reserve Bank of New York has highlighted the need for market par-

---

[2] David Folkerts-Landau and Alfred Steinherr, "The Wild Beast of Derivatives: To Be Chained Up, Fenced In or Tamed," IMF Staff Papers, 1994.

ticipants to establish independent risk-management staff, develop rigorous measurements and analytical capabilities and, in particular, to ensure a strong internal control capability.

> Given that virtually all of the most serious trading-related losses have involved internal control breakdowns, I am convinced that a substantial commitment of monetary and human resources to internal controls earns a high rate of return for dealers and end-users alike.[3]

One effect of all of this has been to shift the operational centre of gravity within banks. The internal audit/compliance functions have moved closer to centre stage. Concurrently, the responsibilities of the external auditor to the bank (their client), and to the authorities, have been redefined. This is of major strategic significance to individual banks, and to the banking system.

The essential value and purpose of internal controls — to strengthen the institutions through more robust, transparent and informed controls — is not in doubt. Much work, however, remains to be done. All of the participants are still on a steep learning curve during a period of unprecedented change in banking and in the capital markets.

What is less clear is whether the internal control systems now in place in most banks — an amalgamation of statutory, prudential and (post-Cadbury) voluntary codes, *overlaid on the banks' own financial controls* — is efficient and cost effective. Does it strike the right balance, in terms of facilitating, on the one hand, good governance and, on the other hand, innovation and competition? Or do the controls, reflecting the overlapping priorities of the supervisory authorities and the banks, impose an excessively costly burden on the banks, which ultimately impacts on the public. Equally, does the integration in the UK of the reporting accountant into the compliance regime enhance banks' internal controls? Or, given the extent to which systems have been upgraded both technologically and in terms of internal reporting arrangements, is the reporting account-

---

[3] W. J. McDonagh "The Derivatives Angst" *Financial Times*, 15th August, 1994.

ant a costly and unnecessary burden on banks? Does the compliance system, within which external auditors have a statutory responsibility to the authorities, distort the traditional relationship with their client, the banks?

Underlying all of this is the fact that there is a difference in "culture" between the banker and the auditor. This has been well summarised by one authority: "Banking is about taking risks. Auditors (generally not perceived as natural risk takers) need to understand that without taking risks, bankers cannot make money".[4] The important point here, of course, is that such risk-taking is *informed*. This goes to the heart of the role of banks in financial intermediation. For this reason banks have, in recent years, invested very significantly in developing new methodologies, procedures and controls to help identify, quantify and manage risk.

There is an evident and pressing need for a dialogue on these and related issues. The purpose of this collection of papers is to facilitate such a dialogue. It brings together — for the first time — the perspectives of the banks, the supervisory authorities and the accountant/auditor. It provides a critique of the role of internal controls in the computerised environment of banks, which can be expected to become progressively more IT-driven. It examines how the *nature* of internal controls in banking have been changed and refined and how this has impacted on organisational and management structures. The main focus is on the UK banking system but the analysis has a much wider relevance.

The first paper, by Anthony Walsh, places the operation and application of internal controls firmly in the context of information technology which is, in effect, re-engineering the business of banking. The impact of IT on the Internal Audit function, for example, in terms of the need for new skills in order to participate in systems development, is compelling.[5] Walsh ex-

[4] Brendan Nelson "Bank Auditing: Is It Still Worth the Risk?" In "Banking Supervision after BCCI", LSE Financial Markets Seminar, London 24th May, 1993.
[5] See, for example, I. Howley "Impact of Technology on Internal Auditing in Banking" — *Irish Banking Review*, Summer, 1993.

amines the ways in which the development of computerised systems generates new risks and the consequential need to adapt internal controls to this new environment. He points out, inter alia, that "in response to the complexity of the [banking] environment, the establishment of strong internal control in a bank's computer system demands an approach which is both wide-ranging and inter-related". Importantly, he argues that many failures in the internal control of banks' computer systems have been traced to ambiguity regarding *responsibility* for internal control which should ultimately be vested in the Board. In relation to the internal audit function, Walsh notes that, if its independence is not to be compromised, it cannot be part of the *formal* framework for contributing a bank's computer system. But it can *reinforce* control by, for example, monitoring compliance with standards. This is likely to be particularly productive in the computerised banking environment because the range and diversity of controls can cause "control fatigue" amongst users and computer specialists.

The following two papers, by John Mogg and Brian Quinn, provide an authoritative supervisory perspective. In Chapter 2, Mogg, the Director-General of DGXV, discusses the wide-ranging nature of the EU Commission's response to the BCCI collapse. This is, indeed, a text-book case of how, in the absence of effective internal controls and a compliance "culture", fraud and dissimulation will inevitably flourish. Mogg sets out the ways in which the wider EU supervisory/compliance regime — within which internal controls operate — has been adapted to take account of the lessons of BCCI.

Brian Quinn, Executive Director in charge of Supervision at the Bank of England, shows in Chapter 3 how the development of the UK banking system, including successive crises, has contributed to a growing awareness of the importance of internal controls and, also, helped define its nature, as set out in the Banking Act, 1987 and subsequently elaborated in successive guidelines on internal controls in banking. His paper provides an insight into the practical operation of internal controls in the UK, including the respective roles of the internal and external audit functions, and, importantly, a supervisor's perspective on the costs of such controls, including the reporting accountant regime, to the banks. The overriding need is for an institution to develop, not just formal systems which, as he points out, are all too often "paper tigers", but rather a control "culture" which is ultimately what "separates the men from the boys".

The pathology of internal controls — their precise nature and how they relate to other functions in the bank — vary, depending on the size of the individual bank, its corporate status (whether, for example it is a parent or subsidiary) as well as, for example, the corporate ethos. Chapters 4, 5, and 6, provide profiles of the development, and practical functioning, of internal controls in three quite different banking groups.

In Chapter 4, Graham Leese outlines the role of Group Audit within NatWest. He examines the internal control functions from the perspective of Group Audit, which, inter alia, monitors the adequacy and effectiveness of key controls. His paper demonstrates clearly the practical importance of controls — "we regard a control as any action taken by management to enhance the likelihood that established goals will be met" — in terms of organisational strategy and efficiency.

Control systems in NatWest have adapted in response to external influences — notably the Cadbury and Bingham reports and, also, the inputs from the reporting accountants responsible to the Bank of England — and also an internal dynamic. In relation to the latter, changes in internal reporting arrangements designed to strengthen the Group Audit function are of particular significance. At the core of the evolution of the Group Audit function has been the transition from an inspection-based approach (traditional policing) to a new emphasis on risk and systems-based auditing. This is, broadly, the pattern right across the industry.

In Chapter 5, John Trethowan reviews the financial control systems of the Northern Bank Group (NBG), a subsidiary of the National Australia Bank. The internal control function is encompassed, within the NBG Group, across the finance, credit bureau and compliance functions. Two factors, in particular, shape the nature of the internal control function. Firstly, the diversification by the NBG in recent years into financial services, which involve compliance requirements, under the Securities and Investment Bank (SIB), *additional* to those involved in banking. This highlights the increasing complexity of developing an appropriate compliance system. Secondly, and more importantly, the role of the parent bank, which has an active involvement in monitoring developments in its subsidiaries. The paper also emphasises the role of the Executive Board in the implementation of internal controls through, for example, the Audit Committee which internal audit and finance functions, as well as external auditors, attend.

In Chapter 6, the theme of risk control is again taken up. Allied Irish Banks (AIB) is one of the two dominant groups (the other is the Bank of Ireland) within the Irish banking market, with an international presence. Cyril Bennett, responsible for treasury risk control with AIB Group Treasury, provides a practical guide to the development of an organisational risk control system. Bennett argues that:

> no single risk management approach or commercial philosophy will insulate a financial institution from the effects of unexpected events on an ongoing basis. However, good management practice and business-focused controls are likely to afford long-term protection to an organisation. Furthermore, they are the essential core values/mechanisms required *to facilitate commercial risk taking in the context of uncertain markets* (emphasis added).

Bennett emphasises the need for developing "a risk-resilient organisation" characterised by a well-defined "risk culture" operating within an appropriate organisational structure. He also addresses the key issue of "the needs of regulators versus the needs of management and whether regulation imposes an unnecessary and heavy cost on financial institutions".

Chapter 7 addresses the issue of internal controls in banking from the perspective of the external auditor/reporting accountant. The starting point of the analysis by Steve Almond of Touche Ross is, quite simply, that there are (as the Courts found in *P. W. vs. BCCI*) "public interest" factors which cause banks to be subject to a significantly higher degree of independent examination than any other business sector. While internal controls in banks may — or may not — be that much more effective than elsewhere in corporate UK, the *demands* for well developed internal controls are, he argues, that much greater. Almond draws an important distinction between the complementary, but distinct, roles of external auditor and reporting accountant. Both — especially the latter — have been shaped by the evolution of the Bank of England's guidelines on the internal control function. And both are, he points out, increasingly vulnerable to a number of pressures, including a more litigious environment and an "expectation gap", whereby third parties have assumed that a bank's internal controls must be sound because they are subject to external audit.

Among the key points that Almond highlights, two merit particular emphasis. First, in addressing the issue of what constitutes "best practice" in relation to internal controls, he echoes Brian Quinn's thesis in asserting that "it doesn't matter how detached or precise a system of controls is, if a bank's management lacks integrity or professional skill and judgement". In this sense, he argues that the internal control environment must be compatible with the bank's "corporate culture". Second, he acknowledges the impact that the growth in the compliance function is having on the business of banking. He bluntly points out that:

> to counter the credit risk minefield . . . some banks have promoted the function of "the back office credit guru", to the point where he is a greater challenge than the external competition for the marketing loan office seeking to write new business.

This, and a number of other themes, are taken up in the concluding chapter, which seeks to identify some of the more important issues relating to the development of the internal control function in banks and their impact on operational efficiency and good governance in banking. It sets out some of the key questions which need to be addressed in what, hopefully, will be an active research-informed, as well as highly practical, dialogue on the role of internal controls in the banking environment of the 1990s.

1

INTERNAL CONTROL IN THE COMPUTERISED BANKING ENVIRONMENT

Anthony Walsh

Dean, Dublin City University
Business School

INTRODUCTION

When finally arrested, a particularly successful bank robber of the 1930s was asked why he targeted banks. He replied, "that's where they keep the money". This reply still has implications today for those involved with computer systems in banks and financial institutions. Money is still "kept" in banks, not just in safes but, more significantly, as magnetic pulses on computer files. Furthermore, this money is transmitted as electronic messages between banks and their clients and can be spent when received as readily as cash. So, just as bank safes were the targets of bank robbers of old, banks' computer systems and transmission lines are increasingly the targets of today's criminals.

Computer technology has widened the range of security threats to which banks must respond. It has also dramatically increased the speed at which they must be capable of responding, and the likely loss per security incident. Although a small number of spectacular cases have been reported in the media, it is widely believed that the losses from most cases of computer fraud in banks go unreported. As a result, it is not easy to estimate the losses suffered by banks through computer-related fraud. The evidence in relation to US banks points to very significant losses arising from fraud. There is very little information available on the losses to European banks through computer fraud or unintentional error.

INTERNAL CONTROL

According to Sawyer (1964):

> Control comprises all the means devised by a company to direct, restrain, govern, and check upon its various activities for the purpose of seeing that company objectives are met. The means of control include, but are not limited to, form of organisation, policies, systems, procedures, instructions, standards, committees, charts of account, forecasts, budgets, schedules, reports, records, check-lists, methods, devices, and internal auditing.

Chambers et al (1987, p. 46) see no essential difference between the internal control of the accountant and auditor and the management control of the management theorists, but note that control overlaps and coalesces with the other functions of management so that it is impossible to think of control in isolation from planning, organising, staffing, directing and co-ordinating.

INTERNAL CONTROL AND THE COMPUTER

The objectives and essential characteristics of internal control do not change with the method of information processing. However, when data are processed by computer, the environment becomes more complex and wide-ranging. It encompasses traditional disciplines, such as accounting and banking, as well as new elements such as hardware, systems and application software and specialist computing staff. Many of the characteristics of this environment can increase the potential for the undermining of internal control. The characteristics of the computerised environment with particular impact on internal control are now briefly examined.

Concentration of Duties

Computer systems tend to concentrate the information processing activities traditionally dispersed throughout a bank into the hands of fewer staff, making it more difficult to achieve the segregation of duties which underpins internal control. It is not surprising, therefore, that most computer-related fraud in banks has been perpetrated by employees.

Reliance on Computer Systems

In the computerised environment, a bank rapidly becomes reliant on the computer system to carry out its business. There is a danger that severe interruption of operations, often involving significant financial loss, will result if the computer system breaks down or is destroyed.

Open Access to Information

Logical access to all the information on a computer system is potentially widely available through terminals and other computers to which the system is networked. Furthermore, with the use of telebanking applications, automatic teller machines (ATMs), electronic funds transfer (EFT) and electronic data interchange (EDI), the potential for unauthorised logical access to a computer system from a wide variety of outside locations is increased. This can lead to unauthorised reading or alteration of data and to theft and embezzlement.

Complexity

The complexity and rate of change of many computer systems introduce their own subtle but real internal control issues. In spite of internal control and security experts preaching a more dynamic approach, there is evidence of a reactive approach to internal control in computer systems with control and audit models and techniques lagging behind technological advances. Senior management is sometimes not perceived as being committed to control measures and may not allocate sufficient resources to them. Lack of commitment on the part of senior management may stem from lack of understanding, or even fear, of computing.

Reduction in Intermediate Review

Bank staff are no longer involved in many processing aspects of computerised systems. There is a danger that the intermediate reasonableness checking, which is carried out both formally and informally in manual systems by staff who are familiar with the transactions being processed, disappears when computer processing is introduced.

Data Conversion

A great deal of information still has to be converted from source documents to magnetic media in a banking environment. This process can give rise to errors.

Knock-on Effect

With computerisation comes a more integrated approach to the processing of banking transactions. One item of input updates many files and may result in the automatic initiation of other transactions. Where there is an input error, many records may be corrupted and erroneous transactions initiated.

Control in the Hands of Third Parties

Because a bank relies on hardware and software which is designed and produced outside the organisation, there is a danger that internal control in its computer-based systems is determined by third parties.

THE BASIS FOR CONTROL

In response to the complexity and variety of the environment, the establishment of strong internal control in a bank's computer systems demands an approach which is both wide-ranging and integrated. It must be wide-ranging in that hardware, software and specialist staff are not just targets of control but become intrinsic components of the control framework itself. It must be integrated because the range of characteristics of the computerised environment which impacts on internal control (such as those discussed above) would undermine an approach which stressed certain areas of control and neglected others.

Many failures in the internal control of banks' computer systems have been traced to ambiguity regarding responsibility for internal control. In fact, there is much disagreement both in the literature and in practice as to who should be responsible for internal control at the operational level (including the division of responsibilities between "users" and "computer specialists" — still an issue in banks in spite of the growth of distributed processing). What is imperative in practice is that responsibility for all aspects of internal control be clearly established and documented without ambiguity, both at the management and operational levels. Some banks establish special units to establish and document responsibility for control while others perform the same function through a committee drawn from users, computer specialists and the human resource management department.

Ultimately, management responsibility for internal control (whether exercised through a unit or committee) should be vested in a member (or members) of the board. If such responsibility resides below this level, it is unlikely that all levels of managers and employees within the bank will give internal control the attention which it merits.

The continuous process of review of responsibility for and the scope of the internal control framework, together with the reviews carried out by the internal control function, is part of the process by which control systems anticipate and adapt to changing circumstances and risks.

Expenditure on internal control should be considered in a cost-benefit context. The risks associated with the computerised system (for example, loss of assets, such as the computer or debtors files; delayed processing) need to be identified and costed. The likelihood of the occurrence of each identified risk then needs to be assessed and, from this information, an annual expected loss may be estimated. Annual expenditure on each internal control measure (for example, acquisition of back-up hardware or security software) may then be considered in the light of the net annual expected loss eliminated.

Formal statistical models which seek to optimise net benefit from internal control activity have a role to play and can give real insights to internal control systems design in banks. But it must be remembered that such models have limitations. For example, there are significant inaccuracies implicit in estimating the probability of occurrence of risks (especially probabilities associated with events occurring very infrequently). The costs and benefits of events are often difficult to estimate. Many are, of their nature, intangible (for example, loss of customer goodwill through errors or poor service). The cumulative effects of these inaccuracies may be great. Nevertheless, attempting to identify net benefit from control activity (with or without optimisation routines) helps highlight controls capable of being replaced with more cost-effective ones.

Formal cost-benefit models should be used as an aid to (and not a substitute for) the judgement and decision-making of managers experienced in both banking and internal control.

CONTROL FRAMEWORK FOR COMPUTER SYSTEMS

We will now briefly examine a framework which highlights the range and depth of control activity required to provide effective internal control in a computerised banking environment. The framework consists of six categories of internal controls:

General Controls
1. Organisational and Administrative Controls
2. Continuity of Processing
3. Personal User Security
4. Controls over Systems Development

Application Controls
5. Input Controls
6. Processing and Output Controls

Organisational and Administrative Controls

Organisational and administrative controls seek to ensure that the organisation's structure and the way in which work is executed and documented contribute to the integrity and reliability of the computer system and the safeguarding of assets of the bank.

The organisation structure should be designed with as clear a distinction as possible between specialist computing staff and users. Within the computing function, management responsibility for activities with conflicting priorities (for example, operations, systems development and media librarianship) should be separated. There should be constructive supervision of both users and specialist computing staff.

In addition to the organisation structure's contribution to internal control, there should be separation at an operational level of those activities which, when together, provide scope for negligence or fraud (for example, record keeping, custody of assets and programming). Related to separation of operational duties are the physical controls which guarantee that the separation is achieved. Particular emphasis should be given to preventing unauthorised access to the computer room or the magnetic media library.

Continuity of Processing

This category of controls aims to prevent loss of data, to provide continuity of processing and protect against financial loss in the event of computer failure.

Shorter-term failure can arise from human error or from failure of hardware, software or services. Controls centre on, first, minimising the likelihood of failure through effective staff training, preventive maintenance, a controlled computer environment and back-up services, and, second, guarding against data loss if failure does occur. The latter is usually achieved through software-based logs of all transactions. The logs are used to reconstruct records or files affected by computer failure.

Longer-term failure can result from accidental or deliberate destruction of hardware, software or services, or from strikes among key staff. Again, controls are aimed, first, at minimising the likelihood of destruction through, for example, secure siting of computer hardware, fire-detection and fire-fighting equipment, and good human resource management. The second line of defence focuses on preventing data loss and securing continuity of computer processing. Data loss is avoided by making certain that copies of datafiles, software and documentation are stored in a remote location. Continuity of processing in a disaster situation is achieved mainly through strategic dispersal of computer hardware or through the acquisition of redundant hardware at back-up locations. The level of hardware redundancy should be decided in a cost-benefit context and should reflect the reliance of the bank's business operations on the computer system. Disaster plans are useful only if well documented and tested. Protection against the cost of replacing computer equipment and the consequential loss of revised working arrangements and data reconstruction should be addressed as part of the bank's insurance strategy.

Personal User Security

Personal user security is designed to prevent or detect unauthorised logical access from any source (for example, through in-house or remote terminals or interference with transmission links) to the bank's computer system, its data and software.

Software-based limitation of access is the backbone of personal user security. All users of the computer system should have to identify themselves. Depending on the sensitivity of the processing action, the identification could be by identity number and password or by more sophisticated techniques such as smart cards, voice or fingerprint recognition. Once users have gained access to the system as a whole, their processing actions in relation to data and programs should be limited by security software to those for which they are authorised. The range of processing actions for which each user is authorised should be minimised. The value of security software is greatly enhanced when combined with additional control features. Examples of these additional features are the limitation of certain processing actions (for example, bad debt write-off) to designated terminals, disconnecting terminals when a number of incorrect passwords have been entered through it, and management review of software-generated reports of processing actions.

Because of the volume and value of the cash and cash equivalents which they control, ATM and EFT systems pose particular control problems. The management of a bank may have to be willing to trade off some reduction in the efficiency of these systems against increased security. The security of each subsystem within the overall ATM or EFT system (for example, boundaries, communication, database and output) must be evaluated as the security of an ATM or EFT system is only as strong as its weakest link. The potential rewards make it well worth the time of fraudsters to detect and exploit any weak link.

On-going review and management of software- and hardware-based controls (such as the encryption/decryption processes used in data transmission, message authentication controls and password/PIN management systems), are necessary to underpin internal control of ATM and EFT systems. The vast majority of ATM and EFT frauds are perpetrated by organisational insiders. A dynamic and multi-faceted approach to control — in which controls themselves are regarded as assets in their own right which have to be protected — is of particular importance when combating potential fraud and negligence from insiders.

Controls Over Systems Development

These controls are designed to guarantee that the bank's software is authorised, developed or purchased in a manner which contributes to good internal control.

These objectives are achieved by formulating, documenting and enforcing standards for the authorisation and implementation of each stage of the bank's systems development cycle (including initial investigation, systems analysis, programming and program purchase, acceptance testing, implementation and systems documentation). Development work should be carried out in accordance with internationally accepted methodologies. Standards should address systems auditability and audit trail, interface with security software, input, processing and output controls and the impact of the new application on provisions for continuity of processing and organisational controls.

Input Controls

Input controls seek to protect the bank's computer system from unauthorised, inaccurate, or incomplete input data.

Programmed controls incorporated into each application program play a pivotal role in achieving this objective. These controls should examine each item of input for conformity with predetermined criteria and input not conforming should be rejected or selected out for further examination. Among the programmed controls used on input are check digits on codes, range and limit checks and completeness tests.

Processing and Output Controls

The objectives of this category of control are to assure the accuracy of processing and the security of output.

Again, software-based controls underpin the accuracy of computer processing. These controls include file label checking (which ensures that the correct files are processed), programme to programme and cycle controls (which check that the balances brought forward at each stage of processing are correct), record and block controls (which check that the number of records on a file is as expected and that no records have been lost or incorrectly added).

Both blank and completed computer output which is in the form of negotiable instruments should be held in safe custody, should be pre-numbered and its issue strictly controlled. Such instruments over a certain value should be countersigned outside the department in which it is printed.

ROLE OF INTERNAL AUDIT

Internal audit is an independent appraisal function within the organisation. If its independence, which is critical to its longer-term value, is not to be compromised, internal audit cannot be part of the formal framework for controlling a bank's computer system. Nevertheless, a bank's internal audit function reinforces control. It does this, *inter alia,* by monitoring compliance with standards, testing that major controls are working and verifying the accuracy of processing and output.

Monitoring of compliance with standards is particularly productive in the computer environment because the range and diversity of controls can introduce control fatigue among users and computing specialists. Without understanding the potential control implication for the computer system, users may be tempted to circumvent control measures in the interests of what they perceive to be operational efficiency.

In all but the smallest banking institutions, it is difficult to see how management could have any confidence in the internal control of its computer system without a properly resourced and independent internal audit function. (The role of the internal control function within the bank is discussed in detail by Graham Leese in Chapter 4).

CONCLUSION

Banks face stiff competition in the marketplace to gain and hold business in an environment which has changed beyond recognition since the 1970s. Information technology plays a central role in the strategic and tactical responses of most banks to this competitive situation. First, in order to reduce their cost base, banks are continuing to extend the use of computers into areas that are labour-intensive. Second, banks are competing for corporate and domestic customers on the basis of the range and quality of the computerised services they can provide. The computerised services offered include EFT, EDI, on-line exchange- and interest-rate management systems, telebanking, ATM, and "smart" credit card facilities.

In summary, it is becoming more and more difficult to conceive of an element of banking services or systems that does not rely on computers.

At the same time, the computer literacy, not just of the general population but also of the criminal fraternity, is rising inexorably as is the availability and sophistication of personal computers.

The combination of these factors means that the value of assets and liabilities controlled by banks' computer systems is increasing as is the range of risks of fraud and unintentional loss to which the systems are vulnerable. This, of course, has far-reaching implications for both the banks themselves and for regulators.

For the banks, expenditure on internal control measures will inevitably rise to counter the additional risks. Perhaps more importantly, the level of attention and priority given to control by senior management, including executive and non-executive directors, will have to be intensified. The highest standards of internal control at the operational level, essential in banking computer systems, can only be achieved within a control climate which is established and managed from the highest echelons of management.

Regulatory authorities may need to become more specific and prescriptive in relation to the internal control systems required in banks. (The Bank of England's current approach to overseeing assessing internal control in banks is discussed by Brian Quinn in Chapter 3). Ultimately, it may be necessary to require directors to certify compliance with internal control standards and to hold them legally responsible when their bank is found to have inadequate standards of internal control. Ultimately, such specific and unambiguous linkage of director responsibility (and liability) to internal control may be required to guarantee top management support for excellence in internal control.

This approach may appear draconian but it must be remembered that the stakes are very high. The potential for growth in the banking sector as a whole is currently quite limited. It is not difficult to envisage a scenario in which an individual bank might be tempted, in order to gain short-term competitive advantage through information technology, to sacrifice internal control standards. Such a scenario could easily lead to losses which would threaten the existence of even quite a large bank. It might also damage public confidence in the industry.

REFERENCES

L. B. Sawyer, "The Anatomy of Control", *The Internal Auditor,* Spring 1964, p. 15.

A. D. Chambers, G. M. Selim and G. Vinten, *Internal Auditing,* London: Pitman, 1987.

2

INTERNAL CONTROLS:
THE EC RESPONSE TO BCCI

John F. Mogg
Director-General EU Commission DG XV
(Internal Market and Financial Services)

INTRODUCTION

On 5th July, 1991, at the instigation of the Bank of England, the Bank of Credit and Commerce International (BCCI) was closed down in a co-ordinated action by banking supervisors in many financial centres because of fraud on a massive and global scale. There was considerable public awareness stemming from the losses of depositors and from fears of a crisis of confidence in the banking industry.

The major banking supervisors therefore engaged in studies in order to analyse the BCCI collapse and draw lessons from it for improving the efficiency of the supervision. Thus, the Basle Committee for Banking Supervision (of the G10 States) produced "minimum standards for the supervision of international banking groups and their cross-border establishments". Moreover, at EC level, the Banking Advisory Committee (where all EC Member States' banking supervisory authorities are represented) considered, during its 1991-92 meetings, the question of whether, in the light of the BCCI closure, the supervisory rules in force or to be adopted at Community level were sufficient to prevent a recurrence of similar incidents and, as far as possible, to provide the supervisory authorities with the necessary instruments and powers to combat them more effectively.

The sub-committee on banking supervision of the Committee of Governors of EC Central Banks, as well as Lord Justice Bingham — acting for the UK government and the Bank of England — also examined the implications of the BCCI case and completed studies and reports.

These four enquiries reached similar conclusions in the analysis of the BCCI collapse and its consequences for the EC Directives concerning banking supervision.

First, the BCCI case was able to develop because of a deliberately opaque organisational structure devised by those in charge of the bank *so that* they could carry out a massive fraud, accompanied by poor banking practice.

Second, the system of home country control and consolidated supervision set up by the relevant EC Directives (i.e. Second Banking Co-ordination Directive (89/646/EEC) and Consolidated Supervision Directive (92/30/EEC)) is essentially sound and does not need major review. However, as these reports suggest, some clarification and at times some reinforcement of banking supervision appeared necessary. That is why, in order to respond to public anxieties over the BCCI case, the Commission decided to take appropriate measures to this end, not only affecting rules to improve banking supervision, but also the way the relevant authorities supervise insurance companies and investment firms. The Commission's proposals for a Council Directive (a "BCCI Directive") amending the Co-ordination Directives of these undertakings, dated 28th July, 1993[1], forms the keystone of these Community measures.

ANALYSIS OF THE BCCI COLLAPSE

Since 1972 — the year BCCI was set up — this bank ballooned into a group whose complexity and fragmentation between worldwide financial centres prevented any prudential authority from exercising effective supervision. This fact, and the close links with some customers who could put large deposits

---

[1] An amended proposal of this Directive was presented to the European Council and European Parliament on 30th November 1994 and is currently awaiting approval.

at its disposal as well as take advantage of unlimited unrecorded loans, allowed some executives (and shareholders) to organise fraud on a large scale. And, also, to dissimulate their poor banking practice. It was the combination of these factors which finally led BCCI to bankruptcy.

Opaqueness of the BCCI Structure

The BCCI structure was tailored in such an intricate way as to allow the Group to present a facade of opaqueness when challenged by regulators. This same opaqueness allowed hidden, and often illegal, cross-share transactions among participators. The structure of the BCCI Group when it was closed down is set out on the following page.

This already complex, but also incomplete, representation of the BCCI structure clearly reveals the worldwide fragmentation of the group which caused many prudential supervision problems.

First, the holding company was, for practical purposes, unregulated. Second, operations were split between different centres, which involved the following consequences: (a) maximum use of banking secrecy, especially in loosely-regulated off-shore centres; (b) dispersion of regulatory responsibilities within the College of Regulators (i.e. Cayman Islands, France, Hong Kong, Luxembourg, Spain, Switzerland, UAE and UK); and (c) absence of consolidated supervision. Third, the head office was separated from the shareholders, the countries of operations and the registered office.

The BCCI structure was also complicated by its various participations in many companies. As this structure was not transparent, most of these participations were not known with certainty. Nevertheless, it appears that some of these companies were offshoots of BCCI (like — apparently — ICIC, a Cayman-based company, purchaser of Bank of America's stake in BCCI by the beginning of the 1980s) in order to allow the bank to acquire its own shares and to bypass legislative controls. Others belonged to BCCI customers with whom specific — and mostly secret — agreements were concluded, in order to facilitate some of BCCI's activities with those of such customers. As a result of these cross-share participations, it seems that BCCI took secret and illegal control of First American Bank as well as stakes, through nominees, in other US-based banks, without complying with US regulations. However, these infringements played only a very small role in the overall BCCI fraud.

Figure 2.1: Structure of the BCCI Group

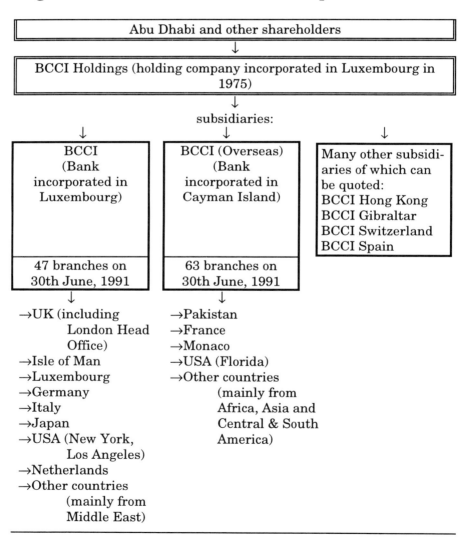

Fraud and Dissimulation of BCCI Poor Banking Practice

Owing to the absence of effective prudential supervision, BCCI managers operated a policy of fraud on a large scale by dissimulating it through a complex manipulation of accounts.

It is now very clear that BCCI, in addition to its illegal acquisitions, was involved in many illicit transactions as well as illegal traffic of different funds (drugs, arms, prostitution, etc.). Among others, BCCI, through a sophisticated system of untraceable back-to-back loans, not only laundered money but also gave the traffickers the opportunity to transfer it to the country of their choice thanks to its worldwide network which prevented the judicial authorities from easily retracing the origin of funds.

The BCCI structure also helped some of its managers to conceal poor banking practice. As BCCI was largely involved in an unlimited speculative trading activity and had no large exposures limits built into its loans policy, the executives were rapidly forced to resort to manipulation to cover up mounting losses. The bank used to sell option contracts to roll the massive treasury losses from one year to the next. But the most commonly used technique to conceal the losses was to split the activities into two sets of accounts. One set recorded the normal operations while the other was run by executives who were using clients' accounts by stealing money from them, transferring it to third party banks, redepositing it in BCCI without indicating its origin and recording this "incoming" money as fresh deposits. The clients' accounts were finally balanced by manufacturing artificial loans to them or by taking in deposits without recording them on the bank's books.

In addition, as many transactions were done on a verbal basis, some new deposits were not recorded and used to cover losses. All these manipulations explain the difficulties that the liquidators now have to face in order to evaluate the true worth of assets and liabilities. The underlying reasons for these difficulties is that, in practice, a balance sheet on a consolidated basis never existed. This largely reflects the non-transparent nature of the bank's operations and the fact that it was already operating in this manner well *before* the drawing-up, and implementation, of BIS and EU standards in relation to consolidation.

COMMUNITY MEASURES TO REINFORCE SUPERVISION OF THE FINANCIAL SECTOR — AND PREVENT ANOTHER BCCI CASE

This analysis of the BCCI affair clearly shows that measures, additional to those already existing, needed to be taken in order to eliminate the opaqueness of financial structures and, on the basis of a clear organisation, to strengthen co-operation between all bodies or persons involved in the supervision of such complex financial structures. The aim must be to ensure that any fraud or poor practice can be detected as soon as possible through a mutual exchange of information between these different competent bodies. In the light of this, the Commission decided to propose such a Directive on 28th July, 1993, for these purposes amending Council Directives 77/780/EEC and 89/646/EEC in the field of credit institutions, Council Directives 73/239/EEC and 92/49/EEC in the field of non-life insurance, Council Directives 79/267/EEC and 92/96/EEC in the field of life assurance, and Council Directive 93/22/EEC in the field of investment firms, in order to reinforce prudential supervision.

Measures on Group Structure

The proposed Directive aims at amending the main Co-ordination Directives which lay down the basis of supervision even though other "specialised" Directives, such as the Consolidated Supervision Directive (92/30/EEC) or the Large Exposures Directive (91/121/EEC), also exist. In order to combat the above-quoted opaqueness of financial structures and facilitate their effective supervision, two types of measures have to be taken, as described below.

Transparency of Group Structures

The financial sector Directives envisage the authorisation of a credit institution, an insurance undertaking or an investment firm as an entity in its own right, or, in other words, without reference to the group in which the individual entity might be placed. The only relevant existing rule in this connection is a requirement that "qualifying" shareholders should be suitable persons. This is not, however, sufficient to cover all the different possibilities that could arise. In the light of this, the Commission proposed that where the financial undertaking was part of a group, the group structure should be sufficiently transparent as to enable the financial undertaking itself to be supervised effectively. To this end, sufficient information must be provided to the competent authorities at the moment of initial authorisation, and also on the occasion of any subsequent change to the group structure.

This power is already implicit in the fifth recital to the Consolidated Supervision Directive. The recommendation of both the Banking Advisory Committee (BAC) and the Bingham Report is that this recital should now be transformed into a substantive provision in the text, which is Article 2 of the Commission's proposal. This has recently been acted upon in the UK.

This article contains general provisions with the objective of ensuring greater transparency of group structures. To prevent the creation of non-transparent relationships, competent authorities are empowered to refuse authorisation if they feel it is difficult to carry out effective supervision of financial undertakings because of opaque relationships between different entities. Furthermore, authorities must receive detailed information by the undertakings about the structural organisation of the group. Finally, information must also be provided in case of changes to the structure of the groups.

Location of the Registered Office and Head Office of Financial Institutions

Effective prudential supervision of a financial institution can also be made more difficult if the supervisors cannot maintain effective contact with the management because the real head office is located in a different country to that of incorporation.

It was, therefore, considered necessary and desirable to ensure that the head office of the financial undertaking remains within the same Member State as the registered office. This is designed to enable supervisory authorities to maintain close contact with the financial undertaking's decision-making body. This rule has already been included in the Investment Services Directive (ISD), so that on this point it is only the Banking and Insurance Directives that needed to be modified.

Article 3 of the proposal requires such a location, so that competent authorities may have effective contact with the decision-making bodies of institutions and thus achieve a more direct control than was the case with BCCI, whose head office was in London but which was registered in Luxembourg. The existence of this Article before 1991 could have been sufficient, by itself, to withdraw the licence of the BCCI and close it earlier.

On the basis of this clarified structure, now possible with draft Articles 2 and 3 of the Commission's proposal, a reinforcement of the provisions relating to the exchange of information among supervisory authorities provisions is now also possible.

Measures on Exchange of Information

As the responsibilities of the supervisory authorities are now well defined, it is necessary to strengthen the *co-operation* between these bodies, so that fraud and poor practice can be more easily detected and identified as soon as possible.

Widening of the Possibilities for Supervisory Authorities to Exchange Information

The professional secrecy requirements in all the main Directives for the financial services sector limits the scope for passing on confidential information to a narrowly defined list of permissible recipients. Within this framework, provision is made to ensure that adequate "gateways" exist so that prudential information can be transmitted backwards and forwards between competent authorities and certain other bodies which have been entrusted with specific tasks within each Member State.

Exchange of confidential information for supervisory purposes is already allowed in the Framework Directives (a) between competent authorities and bodies involved in the liquidation of financial undertakings, and (b) between competent authorities and statutory auditors.

The Commission proposal provides that this possibility should be extended to the authorities which supervise the liquidators and the auditors respectively. The purpose of this extension is to enable the competent authorities to check whether the liquidators and/or auditors have been carrying out their duties correctly.

It is also proposed to extend the list of potential recipients of information so as to include company law inspectors and bodies which are responsible for overseeing payment systems and clearing and settlement services. This possibility of exchanging information is important for competent authorities to be able to catch wrongdoers and should be allowed to take place, provided that it is for supervisory purposes only and that conditions of professional secrecy are strictly observed.

Article 4 of the Commission's proposal is the relevant provision. One should note that the need for it is also linked to the Maxwell case. As a matter of fact, as a consequence of this case, the UK requested that financial supervisors be authorised to pass information to the official inspectors charged with examining abuses of company law.

Such a co-operation could help to prevent another BCCI case, as this bank was involved in many infringements of company law (such as, for example, its illicit stakes in US banks).

Role of External Auditors

The relationship between the supervisory authorities and the external auditors of a credit institution, and the duties of these auditors, have been identified as an important lesson from the BCCI case. Both the BAC and the Bingham report recommended that bank auditors should be put under a statutory duty (and not a right) to report relevant information to the supervisory authorities. This provision already exists in the legislation of some Member States, but not others. It is for consideration whether the external auditor's duty to report to the relevant supervisory authority of regulated financial institutions should be made mandatory by way of specific legislation applying only to financial institutions. This is addressed in Article 5 of the Commission's proposal.[2]

Because of auditors' access to financial undertakings' accounts and other essential material, they are in a position to play an important role in the overall supervisory process. This draft article sets out an obligation for statutory auditors of the accounts of companies to inform the competent authorities immediately they become aware of irregularities in a financial institution's affairs. The present wording of the article is very wide so that this information should be conveyed to the authorities as soon as the principles of sound management have been seriously violated.

Draft Articles 4 and 5 now provide a framework within which all relevant authorities can fully co-operate, so that any sign of fraud, infringement, mismanagement or poor practice can be communicated with minimum delay to the competent bodies. The possibility of another BCCI is greatly reduced. One should note that the Money Laundering Directive (91/308/EEC) also makes the perpetration of BCCI-type frauds much more difficult.

CONCLUSION

With this proposal for a reinforcement of the prudential supervision for the whole financial sector, the Commission intends to strengthen the powers of supervisors, making them better equipped to prevent cases of fraud and other irregularities in the financial services sector.

---

[2] In this context, the European Parliament have proposed that the Directive incorporate provisions to protect external auditors from legal action consequent on their compliance in good faith with their responsibilities under these provisions.

The proposed Directive, accordingly, constitutes the cornerstone of the Community's action in the context of the BCCI affair. In addition, however, two other Community measures are also about to be adopted.

Strengthening of International Co-operation between Prudential Supervisors

There is unanimity in all the reports mentioned above that international co-operation between authorities should be strengthened. In this context, the Basle Committee for Banking Supervision issued "minimum standards", which lay down rules for effective consolidated supervision and the co-operation of supervisory authorities. The Community's 1993 Directive on the consolidated supervision of credit institutions also underlined the importance of the strengthening of international co-operation as the only means to meet the objectives of that Directive in cases where a credit institution belongs to a group with entities outside the territory of the Community.

The Directive accordingly provides that the Commission may submit proposals to the Council, either at the request of a Member State or on its own initiative, for the negotiation of agreements with one or more third countries regarding the means of exercising supervision on a consolidated basis. Strengthening international co-operation between prudential authorities must be a priority for everybody. In December, 1993, the Commission was given by the Council a negotiation mandate in order to promote a structure of co-operation with four major third countries, which are Canada, Japan, Switzerland and the US. Some progress has already been made in these negotiations.

Adoption of Directives which Are Linked to the BCCI Liquidation

The BCCI closure involved losses of around US$10 billion, according to some estimates. As a result many depositors of this bank have suffered from serious financial problems and action in the field of liquidation is necessary.

Deposit Guarantee Schemes

The Bingham report states that the proposed EU Directive for a Deposit Guarantee Scheme is of such significance that it is hoped that its adoption will follow hard upon the coming into force of the Second Banking Co-ordination Directive. This Directive was finally adopted on 30th May, 1994. A similar proposal has been adopted by the Commission of the securities sector on 22nd September, 1993.

Winding-up / Liquidation Directive

Since the beginning of 1993, at the instigation, among others, of the Banking Advisory Committee and the Banking Supervision Sub-Committee of the Committee of the EC Central Banks, the Council has started new discussions on the Commission's proposal on the reorganisation and the winding-up of credit institutions and some significant progress has been made.

It will be clear that the EU has been very active in following up the BCCI affair. There is a good chance that, once all the measures suggested by the Commission and the other international forums are in place, such a fraud will never occur again, or, at least, not on the same scale.

3

THE BANK OF ENGLAND AND THE DEVELOPMENT OF INTERNAL CONTROL SYSTEMS

Brian Quinn

Executive Director and Head of
Financial Supervision, Bank of England

As recently as ten years or so ago, internal control systems would not have featured highly in an analysis of banks and their supervision. Of course, control systems existed then, but they were taken for granted. In the intervening years we have learnt, sometimes the hard way, that this subject cannot be taken for granted; it has become much discussed not only in trade journals but more widely, and not just in the banking industry. The Cadbury Report published in 1992 made important references to aspects of internal control systems in the context of all public companies.

This heightened interest has been reflected in a parallel shift of emphasis in the process of banking supervision. I will first explore why internal systems and controls have become more important for the banks themselves, and then proceed to consider in very broad terms what adaptations of supervision have also taken place.

DEVELOPMENTS IN THE BANKS

Any starting point is bound to be arbitrary, but I will choose the period beginning in 1970, when the publication of *Competition and Credit Control* marked the first steps towards a deregulated banking market in the UK, and the boom years of international banking were getting into full swing.

The first manifestation of the new environment for British banks came in the form of the property collapse of the early 1970s affecting mostly smaller banks, but also involving some of our major banks. At about the same time the larger banks were becoming engaged either as arrangers or lenders in a great surge of international credit expansion, initiated by the recycling — as it was then called — of money flowing from the oil producing countries back to the oil consumers.

Although both of these developments, nationally and internationally, led to sizeable shifts in the asset composition of the banking system, the business was still recognisably that of lending. The business of arranging the loans was similarly not fundamentally different from the traditional corporate finance business of the merchant banks. However, traditional credit assessment systems were not well equipped to deal with new forms of concentration, whether in the form of country risk or in the form of counterparty risk through highly articulated national and international inter-bank markets. Although inter-bank markets had always existed, the scale and spread of their development in the 1970s, both in the UK and abroad, was quite striking.

The associated reliance by banks on wholesale money gave rise to a significant need for improved systems and controls in the area of liability and liquidity management, unfortunately realised only too late by many fringe banks in the secondary bank crisis of the mid-1970s. Wholesale money was volatile, being sensitive both to interest rates and to confidence. For banks, financing their activities in the 1970s through these markets demanded a re-examination of the relevant control techniques to measure and manage both the maturity profile and interest rate risk.

In the 1980s and 1990s even more fundamental changes have become apparent. Banks' activities have spread into wholly new areas, especially trading, hitherto largely restricted to foreign exchange. At the same time other, more familiar, activities have become much more specialised.

One of the greatest challenges has undoubtedly been the attempt to combine traditional banking with trading. The former was not only well understood — although it seems not well enough understood to avoid a new round of excessive lending in the late 1980s — but is a relatively slow-moving business. In that sense it is inherently easier to devise and employ the necessary systems and controls.

By contrast, trading moves literally at the speed of sound — and computer-driven trading nearer to the speed of light. To suggest that more responsive risk management tools are necessary is a considerable understatement. Formal systems and controls, although obviously vitally necessary, are not sufficient. The problems that may occur cannot all be anticipated and the strong human element in trading has proven not to be easily susceptible to formal document-based controls.

What is needed in these circumstances is the inculcation of a set of *values* and frame of *mind* throughout the business that will lead to an appropriate response to an unexpected situation. That is always desirable, but it becomes essential in a fast-moving business. Put this way, it becomes much easier to understand why the move by banks into the securities business after the Big Bang in 1986 has caused so many internal difficulties. In only a very few cases has it proved possible to weld together fully-fledged banking and securities businesses without a great deal of pain. The *cultural differences* have been even greater than expected.

In one sense, the trading culture seems to be the stronger since it has had a large-scale and still extending influence on traditional banking. It has led to the risks previously bundled up within a loan being unbundled and manipulated. Fixed-rate lending is switched into floating rate, and vice versa, with collars and caps providing intermediate positions. Loans are bought and sold in secondary markets and securitised. Even traditional banking has become much more technical.

The upshot is that a general banker can no longer hope to understand in any depth all the activities undertaken in his bank. Common sense ceases to be an ally when nothing is common and sense is not enough by itself; and because change has occurred so recently the necessary skills and experience are held in individual specialist areas of each bank and often have not yet permeated top management.

Another feature may seem trite but is not to be underestimated: systems and controls have ceased to be tangible, and persons cannot relate to them in a physical sense. Bookkeeping has been replaced by electronic pulses. Assessment of risk by means of adding up loans has been replaced by rocket science, such as dynamic hedging based on mathematical modelling. On the way, systems and controls too easily become depersonalised and remote. It is less easy for a person affected by one part of them to understand how that part fits into the whole, and it becomes easier for that person to lose respect for them. Walking around the office may seem old-fashioned but it conveyed several important signals. Banks are learning today that remote control can sometimes mean no control.

However, focusing just on the increasing diversity and complexity of banking, and the challenge that poses for the directors and managers responsible for the control of their business, is to miss another important part of the picture: the impact of competition. Before 1970, and even well into the 1970s, life was much cosier for banks, with two relevant consequences. Banks' pricing included larger safety margins against risk, and this provided an extra cushion against failure of internal risk control.

Secondly, there was not the same pressure to gain or retain business, whether by underpricing or over-exposing to risk, as there is now. One illustration of this is the increasing emphasis on control of pricing and costs, representing a sea change from the early 1970s.

As traditional banking has become a mature industry, with limited scope for expansion of demand and other sources of supply, one has either to diversify or to excel to remain profitable. In both cases, *good systems* and *controls and a strong compliance culture* are necessary. The results are evident: a small number of banks have consistently prospered in the last two decades since 1979, almost whatever the state of the economy. Many others have at best stood still and still others have left the sector altogether. Much, perhaps most, of the difference between the more and less successful has been the strength of their systems and controls. That goes well beyond the structure of rule books and exception reports. All too often such formal structures are paper tigers, proving to be too inflexible to cope with new circumstances and thus unreliable and indeed sometimes ignored. It is the *control culture* that tends to separate the men from the boys.

A final factor at work over these years has been the rising standards of *ethics* with which banks have been required to comply — and I do not mean supervisory standards as such, about which I will speak shortly. Like it or not, banks are expected to display generally higher standards of behaviour in conducting their affairs. Activities regarded as perfectly acceptable a few years ago can now draw upon banks severe criticism in the media. Whether this is desirable or not is an issue for another time. What is clear is that banks must take steps to protect their reputation since failure to do so can be disastrous to their business. These steps include introducing the relevant *reporting arrangements*, the proper *guidelines* to staff, the necessary *training* in the recognition of potential problems and the *checking mechanisms* designed to catch the lapses from accepted standards.

This, above all, is where the control culture plays its most important part. The successful banks are those which, year in and year out, combine (a) technical expertise, (b) a clear vision of their role in life and (c) a strong control culture that permeates the whole enterprise.

Employees in these banks know very well what is expected of them and are supported by — not slaves to or constrained by — a positive control ethic.

THE SUPERVISOR'S REACTION

The 1979 Banking Act set no criterion for authorisation which related to systems and controls, nor to internal audit, nor to "high level" controls such as non-executive directors or audit committees, as it was not thought to be an issue requiring specific attention. The rules of banking were thought to be well-known and respected; and in general they were. It was in other areas of the management of deposit-taking that the main risks for depositors were considered more likely to lie.

This proved to be an unduly innocent assumption, but it was not unreasonable at the time. The Act did contain adequate general powers to deal with the system and control weaknesses where it was thought they were most likely to be present, in the smaller institutions which were licensed deposit-takers. It was correctly anticipated that in this population the main difficulty in the systems and control area would be achieving sufficiently independent control of a dominant chief executive in a small business; hence the "four eyes" criterion in Schedule 2 of the 1979 Banking Act.

The failure of Johnson Matthey in 1984 was a rude awakening. It brought home the message that even quite large banks could have life-threatening deficiencies of systems and controls. It was clear that the Bank of England's general powers over recognised banks like Johnson Matthey needed boosting to at least the level of those available over licensed deposit-takers, and that supervision over the control of internal administrative systems was now sufficiently important to be included specifically in the criteria for authorisation.

Both these deficiencies were addressed in the 1987 Banking Act and in the Bank's *Statement of Principles* published shortly afterwards. To be authorised now, a bank must satisfy the Bank of England that it maintains adequate accounting and other records; has adequate systems of control of the business and of its records; has non-executive directors, where appropriate; and has satisfactory arrangements for internal and external audit.

The Bank has supervised compliance with these requirements in two ways. It has sent in its own "review teams" of bankers and accountants, mainly seconded from the major firms; these are proving a valuable resource.

Secondly, using the specification of its power in section 39 of the 1987 Act (see Appendix 1), the Bank has required all banks to provide it with reports covering the adequacy of systems and controls, and of the accuracy of supervisory statistical returns. These reports are prepared by reporting accountants engaged by and paid for by the banks.

This approach was adopted after extensive consultation with the banks and the accountancy profession, and resulted in the issue of guidance notes for reporting accountants. The note on internal control systems did not seek to prescribe a model, but instead set out what they should cover and seek to achieve. Although reporting accountants, relying on these guidance notes, give an opinion whether the internal controls in a bank are adequate, it is definitely not a supervisory opinion — that can be done only by the Bank of England, in relation to its interpretation of the statutory criteria for authorisation.

The reporting accountants' regime has now been in place for five years, and has in many ways supplemented the Bank's own knowledge of institutions' internal systems and controls. We pay careful attention to the reports and have relied on them on numerous occasions in coming to a decision on whether our powers under the Act are exercisable. However, we are still considering ways in which this regime can be better directed and used.

The most common criticism from bankers is that the costs of reporting accountants, which are borne by each bank, outweigh any benefit they receive. I find this a difficult point to respond to. Of course, it is not easy for each bank to have a full picture of the benefit to them, as they do not know what alternative action we might have taken if we had not had a report from accountants. There is no doubt that by one means or another we would have wanted a substitute process since we regard this subject to be too important to ignore. Nor can banks know what would have happened even if we had elected to abandon this technique. Despite it, and despite managements' own best intentions, things do go unexpectedly wrong. Even among the largest and most powerful banks operating in London, deficiencies have been unexpectedly uncovered. This has caused us some concern recently, and we are considering whether there are any lessons to learn.

With respect to the reports on the accuracy of supervisory statistical returns, our earliest instructions for completing these returns were sometimes unclear and occasionally deficient. Much more comprehensive instructions are now given for the more important supervisory reports. The accountants' reports have also thrown up a large number of weaknesses in banks' reporting arrangements leading to some quite major inaccuracies.

As these returns are the bedrock of our process of supervision these can have major implications for, at best, misunderstandings. The arrangements for reporting accountants have therefore been of very great value here.

Nevertheless, we are ready to consider suggestions, supported by reasonable evidence, that greater benefit could be wrung out of the present arrangements. The key clearly continues to be the need for proper communication.

The high point of the process of reports from accountants on systems and controls is the "trilateral meeting", when the bank being reported on, the reporting accountant, and the Bank of England review the contents of the report together. There are bound to be tensions arising from the potentially adversarial relationships between the three parties, and that can and has diminished the amount of communication. I accept that part of the explanation may lie with the way in which the meetings are conducted, as well as their timeliness, and we are trying to make improvements in these areas. But I have to say that some reporting accountants have been less open than is necessary for real communication, due to their nervousness at upsetting their client. That is, I think, a wrong if understandable reaction; everybody, particularly the client, gains from open communication. I am the first to admit that this can also be facilitated by ensuring that supervisors are fully prepared for the trilaterals in the technical sense of understanding the nuances of the reports under consideration.

Not only are reporting accountants nervous about the effects of some of the exchanges of information on their relationship with their client, but that the bank clients are too. We recognise that unnecessary, or at least unwelcome, damage can be done to what should be a co-operative relationship. This issue was closely studied in the preparation for the 1987 Banking Act, when the conclusion was that auditors should have the ability, but not a statutory duty, to report to the Bank of England concerns which related to the ability of their client to meet the criteria for authorisation. The question of the role of the auditor re-emerged in view of the recommendation of

Lord Justice Bingham that this ability to report to the supervisor should be replaced by a statutory duty to do so in specified circumstances.

This proposal has again prompted concern in the banking community about the potential for damaging relationships with their auditors, but I do think this may be overdone. Notwithstanding my earlier remarks, the same fears which were expressed when the 1979 Act was introduced proved to be exaggerated, both as to the damage that was done and the frequency with which these powers were used. I do not expect experience would be much different if a duty were to replace an enabling power.

Secondly, the current arrangements leave the reporting accountant and the auditor in an exposed and unsatisfactory position. They can be placed in a position in which they face a real conflict between their duty of confidentiality to their clients and their powers under the law: the worst of both worlds. We therefore encouraged Lord Justice Bingham to reach his conclusion, and we welcomed its acceptance by the Government. Indeed, the proposal also had the support of the European Commissioner, Sir Leon Brittan. A paper issued by the Auditing Practices Board in 1992 suggested that auditors should actually report to a wider range of "stakeholders" of a company than just the shareholders, and that this could be formally recognised in exchange for a limitation in their exposure to litigation. Other ideas were aired, such as a requirement for the rotation of auditors.

Since 1987, requirements for banks to have sufficient representation of non-executive directors and control of audit — both external and internal — have been introduced. Together, these comprise part of the subject of "high level" controls, which has since then become topical for all public companies, and not just banks.

It is inevitably difficult to generalise on this subject. A large clearing bank will clearly need a range of high level controls which are unsuited to a small banking business with very little distinction between high and low levels of management. The Bank has recognised this both in its 1987 paper on audit committees and in its annual Banking Act reports. The more complex and the bigger the company the greater the case for high level controls. This is why we started our administration of this part of the 1987 Act with the largest UK banks, since it is here that we are best able to begin to assess the control culture in the organisation.

In addition to the supervisor's reaction to the needs of banks to enhance their systems and controls in order to control risks, where the objective is clearly prudential there is another force driving the supervisors — that of public policy expressed more generally. This can take several forms, some of which until recently were thought not to be of any direct relevance to banks and their supervisors. Money laundering is the clearest example, but the prevention of other forms of criminality affecting the financial system represent a rapidly growing area of concern to supervisors, financial institutions and law enforcement agencies.

This aspect of public policy is very much a phenomenon of the mid and late-1980s. Starting with anti-drug and terrorist legislation, it has rapidly acquired an international impulsion from initiatives in OECD, the Basle Supervisors' Committee and the EC. A common response to these concerns has been a focus on the need for reporting and control systems to detect and prevent these abuses of the banking system. I can understand that some banks may find these developments alien and even distasteful. But it is clear to me that the threat to banking systems from these forces is very real and extremely dangerous. We may have to be ready to modify long-held beliefs and practices to meet this challenge. The Bank of England has itself established a Special Investigations Unit with these concerns in mind, and is also supplying the first head of a Financial Fraud Investigation Network which enables information on such activities to be made available to all interested supervisory and criminal prosecution agencies. Of course, care will have to be taken to ensure that this mechanism is applied only to its desired objectives.

CONCLUSION

Banking is, like so may other activities today, becoming ever more complex, faster and subject to rapid change. Survival and success in these circumstances demands good management. That involves not only understanding the business itself and applying the most up-to-date and efficient technology but also entails harnessing that technology to help manage the risks. But of course technology itself, for all its power and sophistication, is not enough. It will assist and deliver only in a benign environment. In banks, that means in an environment in which systems and controls serve and underpin values *already* clearly established and generally accepted.

Banking supervisors, for their part, need to stay up with the times and to reinforce managements' efforts to protect depositors. More and more this means satisfying themselves that systems and controls are in place and being properly and faithfully observed. Auditors are clearly moving increasingly in the same direction. Between us all we may perhaps get it much more often right than wrong. Anything less than that seems to me unlikely to be accepted as an adequate response in today's world.

4

THE ROLE OF GROUP AUDIT

Graham Leese
Manager, Standards & Techniques,
National Westminster Bank

INTRODUCTION

Internal controls within major UK banks have not proved sufficiently robust to prevent well-publicised scandals, glaring own goals and massive bad debts in recent years. The media have played their part in dramatising the sector's problems but why, with so much scrutiny by internal and external auditors, have the banks still managed to find new and interesting ways of arousing public and shareholder anxiety?

A fundamental problem, and possibly the major enemy of internal control, is change. Established internal control procedures can rapidly become redundant in the face of hurried policies, constant reorganisations and poorly implemented technology. Pressures to meet sales targets, outperform competitors, reduce costs or meet tight deadlines often work against a stable, mature and well-controlled environment.

On the other hand, for banks to prosper they have to respond quickly and positively to increasing competition and the more sophisticated demands of customers, shareholders, regulators and employees. Delays due to bureaucracy and over-control can constrain the decision making process and reduce profit-earning potential. Banks must therefore accept that continual change is unavoidable and that greater operating risks are a natural consequence. They need to modify their systems of internal control in line with these changes and to ensure by regular review that they are appropriate to the current operating risks of the business.

In providing its services to management and giving assurances to the Board, the internal audit function must be able to help and not hinder this change process. The function itself must be adaptable and alert and its working practices must allow for the continually changing banking environment and associated risks.

This chapter considers how Group Audit within the National Westminster Bank group (NWB) has responded and is continuing to respond to these demands. It describes how we provide a service to management and the Board, helping them to meet their objectives and to control risks. It also explains our relationships with other internal and external bodies who have similar concerns or responsibilities.

INTERNAL CONTROLS

First, it is important to understand what we mean by internal control. Following the Cadbury Committee's report on the Financial Aspects of Corporate Governance in December 1992, a Working Group, comprising representatives of the accountancy profession and major listed companies, is considering the recommendations relating to internal control and financial reporting. In its interim report of October 1993, the Working Group defined internal control as:

> The whole system of controls, financial or otherwise, established in order to provide reasonable assurance of (a) effective and efficient operations; (b) reliable financial information and reporting; and (c) compliance with laws and regulations.

We regard a control as any action taken by management to enhance the likelihood that established goals will be achieved. Controls will generally be designed to prevent, detect and/or correct some error or failure that could adversely affect the running of an operation or business function. Errors or failures could be unintentional or deliberate and could arise from a whole mass of threats and activities, both within and external to the organisation.

For a company's statement in its Annual Report, the Working Party is proposing that the Directors need only specifically address the *financial* aspects of internal control. A more restricted internal financial control is defined as:

> The internal controls established in order to provide reasonable assurance of the maintenance of proper accounting records and the reliability of financial information used within the business or for publication.

As far as we in Group Audit are concerned, the scope of our work extends to the wider definition and, in the terms of the Cadbury Committee report, our role in relation to internal control could be described as *monitoring* the adequacy and effectiveness of key controls.

The Bank of England has issued its own guidelines on internal control and the particular guidance relating to internal audit is quoted below.

> 1. *Internal audit is an integral part of the internal control system* established and maintained by management and *is distinct* from the primary control function of an inspection department which provides day-to-day control over transactions and operations.

> 2. The existence, scope and objectives of internal audit are dependent upon the judgement of management as to its own needs and duties, the size and structure of the institution and the risks inherent in the business. Important considerations in assessing the effectiveness of internal audit include the scope of its terms of reference, its independence from operational management, its reporting regime and the quality of its staff.

> 3. While the Bank does not consider it appropriate at the present time to prescribe that all authorised institutions have an internal audit, it nevertheless believes that the following secondary control functions could be undertaken by internal audit:

> a. review of accounting and other records and the internal control environment;

> b. review of the appropriateness, scope, efficiency and effectiveness of internal control systems;

   c. detailed testing of transactions and balances and the operation of individual internal controls to ensure that specific
control objectives have been met;

   d. review of the implementation of management policies; and

   e. special investigations for management.

DESCRIPTION OF GROUP AUDIT

Origins

NWB has evolved into a complex organisation with subsidiaries throughout the world and a diversification of financial
services and interests. The risks facing this organisation, both
internal and external, are continually changing and threaten
both short-term profits and the long-term success of the group.
It is, therefore, the stated policy of NWB that a proper internal
audit function should be maintained, providing the Board with
some assurance that significant operating risks are being controlled effectively.

   Group Audit had its origins in domestic retail banking,
where it fulfilled an inspectorate role, regularly visiting
branches and departments to conduct compliance tests of
documented control procedures. Inspectors were generally experienced, high-calibre branch managers seconded to the department and trained to follow a lengthy inspection programme. This approach was justifiable in the once stable and
homogeneous branches, but there was a need for a more flexible approach elsewhere. Inspections were considered to be ineffective at assessing the quality of controls in one-off departments or functions, and they were not designed to cope with
the rapid changes in technology and diversification of banking
business.

   In 1989, following remarks by NWB's reporting accountants
in relation to the Bank of England guidelines (see above), external consultants were employed to review the role of the department. They recommended major changes to strengthen the
independence and professionalism of the internal audit function, including a wider focus on risks affecting the group, a di-

rect reporting line to the Board and an increase in the numbers of professional accountants and internal auditors employed.

These recommendations were approved by the Board and have subsequently been incorporated into our role and responsibilities, described below. The greater emphasis on risk and systems-based auditing was exemplified in the department's change of name from Group Inspection to Group Audit in 1990.

The more direct reporting line to the Executive improved the standing and authority of the department, but the Director of Group Audit also continued to report to the Audit & Compliance Committee (A&CC). This committee consists of non-executive directors and serves to provide shareholders with assurance that risks throughout the group are being recognised and suitably dealt with by executive and senior management.

The A&CC's terms of reference were recently amended to reflect the Code of Best Practice, published as part of the Cadbury Committee's report on the Financial Aspects of Corporate Governance. The Cadbury report was examined by a high level NWB working party and proposals were made to revise standards and comply with the recommendations, throughout the group. However, the impact on Group Audit has not been very significant, given that major steps had already been taken to improve our objectivity and professionalism.

From our perspective, Group Audit and the A&CC have the full support of the Board, which has responded positively to recommendations by the Bank of England, reporting accountants and external auditors.

Objectives

The review of 1990 highlighted the importance of concentrating audit effort on areas of significant risk. New terms of reference were agreed by the Board and the prime objective for the department is now defined as:

> To advise Executive Management and the A&CC on the quality of control over and identification of all significant operating risks within the Group.

Quality of control refers to the adequacy, efficiency and effectiveness of controls. In other words, are the right controls in place to mitigate the significant risks and are they applied effectively at the right time by the right people?

There are many definitions and classifications of risk but, from our perspective, risk is described as "the chance that some event or failure will occur that will ultimately result in financial loss to the business".

For example, loss of reputation through some inadvertent or illegal act could eventually result in loss of income, as well as costs to remedy the situation. Operating risks refer to any risks that could have impact on the operations of the group, apart from those arising as a direct result of strategic decisions made by the Executive. However, Group Audit is not precluded from reviewing the information gathering and analysis processes behind any strategic decision.

Scope

To fulfil its duties to the Board and the NWB A&CC, Group Audit has to ensure it is capable of reviewing all identified operating risks and controls throughout the Group. Our responsibilities therefore extend world-wide and may either take the form of overseas visits by UK-based auditors or may rely on locally appointed audit management and staff in the larger subsidiary companies.

The heads of these subsidiary departments report directly to their local A&CC but they also have a functional reporting line to the Director of Group Audit. The Director has the right to attend all A&CCs throughout the group and may bring major issues to the attention of the parent bank A&CC or members of the Executive.

The report of Lord Justice Bingham on the Bank of Credit and Commerce International (BCCI) repeatedly mentioned the lack of any one country's supervisory powers over BCCI and associated companies and banks. Our global audit responsibilities may therefore give some reassurance to our external auditors, reporting accountants and regulators.

Structure

Group Audit's structure is aligned to that of the group itself, allowing auditors to develop relationships with relevant business managers and to build on their knowledge of local functions and technology. Auditors are required to have a suitable understanding of the business as well as the required technical knowledge and auditing skills. However, there are also the following specialised central functions that have their own portfolio of work, as well as providing technical assistance to other sections and subsidiaries within Group Audit.

Fraud Office

The Fraud Office has a specialised role investigating money laundering and attempted frauds against NWB. Its main objectives are to recover, minimise and prevent losses to NWB, making use of its group-wide network of contacts and links with law enforcement agencies. It also provides training material and regular publications on fraud prevention issues.

Special Matters

Special Matters investigates any irregularities within NWB where staff misdemeanours are suspected. The nature of their work requires them to react quickly to limit any losses and to protect NWB's reputation.

Branch Inspectorate

The Branch Inspectorate still performs inspections on High Street branches, using a prescribed programme of compliance tests, but there is now a greater focus on significant risks and more use of auditing techniques. The role of the inspector is bound to change further in the near future as the UK branch network is being restructured to improve efficiency and customer service. Greater use will be made of specialised service centres and IT systems, reducing the role and responsibilities of individual branches.

Information Systems Audit

This provides technical advice and reviews the controls associated with the IT infrastructure and major applications within NWB.

OPERATING PRACTICES

The majority of work undertaken by Group Audit follows a standard audit approach based on the recommended standards of professional internal and external auditing bodies. This approach is deliberately flexible and set at a high level to allow auditors sufficient freedom to use their skills and judgement to best advantage. There are dangers that risks or irregularities could be missed with too rigid and prescribed an approach.

A typical audit involves appraising the adequacy and effectiveness of internal controls and making recommendations to improve any identified deficiencies. An audit will not specifically address *compliance* with legal and regulatory requirements unless the compliance risks associated with the audit are found to be significant. Reviewing compliance is not therefore a matter of course in an audit, and it is often more effective to audit the particular compliance functions as they affect a number of departments or systems (see also Group Compliance below).

The following description of our working practices is included to help demonstrate how the scope and methods of an internal audit function can benefit internal control, particularly in the context of concerns over banking supervision and corporate governance. Our work also occasionally covers other duties, such as advising on projects or contributing investigative work in connection with group acquisitions.

Risk Assessment and Planning

The selection of a particular department, function or system to audit relies on an understanding of the organisation and its associated risks. Large departments or systems are therefore examined and divided into more manageable audit assignments that both cover the key risks and make best use of available skills and resources. In some cases the audit may focus on the operations of a particular department or system, or perhaps it may cover a function that cuts across various parts of the organisation.

To make the most effective use of limited resources, areas exposed to higher risks are audited more often and in more depth than those with lower risks. Audit plans are therefore based on a risk assessment of each audit, produced using our own risk assessment methodology. Each audit is given a percentage risk rating, which is based on weighted scores for factors relating to financial size, business impact, vulnerability and stability. This rating is then used to prioritise new audits and schedule return visits.

When comparing the relative inherent risks of audits, we generally do not speculate on the quality of internal control, although we would take some account of any history of problems or well-known weaknesses. Failure to control is not in itself a risk and a missing, ineffective or unreliable control should be identified and remedied as part of the audit process. It may not be possible to eliminate an inherent risk but the audit can recommend improved controls to reduce vulnerability.

Each section and subsidiary within Group Audit produces its own audit plans, which are submitted for approval to the Director of Group Audit and the appropriate A&CC. Regular meetings and management information reports to the executive and non-executive directors are used to highlight major problems, show progress against annual plans and explain any significant variances.

Planning Individual Assignments

Each audit assignment is planned in detail to focus on significant risks and to make the most effective and efficient use of resources. The scope and objectives of the audit are formulated after gaining sufficient understanding of the audit subject, including business objectives, high level risks, operating environment and organisation structure. The resources necessary to perform the audit are estimated from previous or similar audits and relate to the complexity of the audit subject and the significance of the risks.

Systems Evaluations

Information is gathered to help evaluate the adequacy of the systems of internal control put in place by management to achieve its business objectives. Evaluation requires judgement by the audit team, who have to determine:

- What are the significant detailed risks?

- What control would be expected to mitigate those risks?

- Are the actual controls in place adequate for the purpose?

- Are there any compensating controls?

By comparing actual and expected controls, any omissions or inadequacies are identified. The key controls, on which reliance has to be placed, are then tested to confirm they are effective and reliable. Testing involves various mixes of observation, enquiry, inspection and computation, although auditors are not expected to rely on enquiry alone.

To help in making these judgements, the systems of control relating to the significant risks are generally documented, using flow charts or narrative notes. Auditing techniques such as computer interrogation and sampling are used to support the tests, and sufficient evidence is collected to support any conclusions and recommendations.

Reporting and Follow-up

At the conclusion of an audit, a report is issued to executive management as well as the operational management involved in the assignment. The aim of the report is to be constructive and to the point, highlighting any major concerns, commenting on the adequacy and effectiveness of key controls and recommending any remedial action or enhancements. The report is discussed fully with operational management, who are asked to produce and agree an action plan. The audit team then follows up the report to confirm that suitable and timely action has been taken.

Reports are reviewed by Group Audit senior management to identify adverse trends or widespread problems that may need to be addressed from a broader perspective or escalated to the Executive. Each report is graded and copies of unsatisfactory reports are sent to the external auditors.

All major concerns are reported to the A&CC through its regular meetings with the Director of Group Audit or, exceptionally, as a matter of urgency. Ideally, members of the A&CC should read all audit reports, or at least the executive summaries, but in practice the sheer number of reports issued makes this prohibitive. The A&CC therefore relies on the Director of Group Audit to escalate major concerns, secure in the knowledge that the external auditors also review our reports and may raise issues independently.

Development Audits

A Development Audit refers to an independent assessment of the controls associated with a major project to develop or enhance a service, product, function or IT system. The scope of a development audit includes one or both of the following:

- An evaluation of the risks and proposed internal controls of the new or enhanced business service, product, function or IT system, to ensure that risks will be adequately mitigated and controlled in live service.

- An appraisal of the project management and systems development processes, to seek assurance that the risks inherent in change are being managed and controlled effectively and that the risks accepted do not outweigh the potential benefits of the development.

Our involvement in any project depends again on the scale of the associated risks. However, we feel that the earlier we are involved the greater the service we can provide. It is far more practical and cost effective to correct potential weaknesses while a product or service is being designed rather than trying to make remedial changes after it has been delivered. This is one of the advantages of internal audit, in that we are part of the organisation and are able to respond quickly to the operational risk situations.

RELATIONSHIPS

Audit & Compliance Committee (A&CC)

The A&CC is made up of non-executive directors, although all Board members receive papers and are entitled to attend meetings. It was formed on the recommendation of the Bank of England in 1977 and was originally known as the Audit Committee.

As mentioned above, the A&CC has recently had its terms of reference slightly amended to reflect the findings of the Cadbury report and its role and responsibilities closely mirror the Cadbury recommendations. The effect on Group Audit's role and authority has been minimal, considering the major improvements that we have already made in recent years.

The Director of Group Audit reports to the parent bank A&CC and attends regular meetings to review the department's plans and any major issues arising from our audits. He also has the right to attend similar committees with subsidiary organisations, who generally arrange their meetings to precede those of the parent bank.

The A&CC meets in private with the external auditors at least once a year and, where considered necessary, the Chairman is authorised by the Board to obtain independent professional advice or to seek information from any employee within the group.

Line Management

The management of risk is an essential feature of successful business activity. The Board and management at all levels throughout the group are therefore responsible for establishing and maintaining appropriate systems of control to help them achieve their objectives and discharge their obligations.

The role of the auditor is not to design or maintain internal controls on behalf of line management but to act as an independent reviewer and advisor on risk and control issues. However, where advice is not acted upon, the Director of Group Audit may deem it necessary to go over the heads of operational management and escalate issues to the Executive or the A&CC.

External Auditors

External auditors are appointed by shareholders and fulfil a statutory duty. They are required to comment openly on a company's financial well being and its compliance with accounting standards. The Cadbury report highlighted a number of areas where their effectiveness could be and is being improved through greater consistency and the tightening of standards, but these areas are outside the scope of this chapter.

The major difference between external and internal auditors relates to their reporting lines and responsibilities. External auditors provide reassurance to the owners of the company, whereas the primary goal of internal auditors is to help internal management and the board to meet their objectives. The Cadbury report sees the internal audit role as an integral part of the monitoring of internal control, although both internal and external auditors are expected to make constructive recommendations and not just to monitor or find fault. We may both also be expected to act on behalf of regulators or assist the A&CC in meeting their obligations.

We maintain a close working relationship with our external auditors and they review our standards and operating practices as well as the reports we generate. They receive copies of all unsatisfactory internal audit reports as a matter of course and working papers are made available on request. We meet regularly to discuss plans and to ensure that the audit effort is co-ordinated and not duplicated. We also occasionally undertake work on their behalf and receive copies of their management letters.

Regulators

The Director of Group Audit meets formally with the Bank of England about four times a year to discuss regulatory and supervisory issues and to review the programme now undertaken by the reporting accountants under the Banking Act 1987. Where appropriate, we undertake work on behalf of the reporting accountants.

As mentioned above, we have responded strongly to the recommendations of the reporting accountants and we comply with the Bank of England's guidelines on internal audit. As an audit function we also wish to ensure through audits and inspections that NWB as a whole complies with statutory and regulatory requirements. We therefore liaise closely with our colleagues in Group Compliance — see below.

Group Compliance

NWB has a separate Group Compliance function that helps to set policy and standards in relation to compliance with legal and regulatory requirements. It also provides a regular monitoring service in key areas and may follow up on issues raised by auditors.

Both departments report to the A&CC and there is regular dialogue between the two directors to ensure that risks and sensitive issues are being adequately covered by the two departments.

Group Risk Policy Committee

In recent years, bearing in mind the concerns leading to the Cadbury and Bingham reports, as well as the effects of the recession, NWB has established a network of risk management committees throughout the group. The general aim of this network of committees is to ensure that all major risks are identified and suitably managed. Lower level committees across the Group report to the Group Risk Policy Committee, which consists of sector chief executives and is chaired by the Chief Executive, Group Risk.

The Group Risk Policy Committee establishes policy relating to key risks issues and deals with both one-off and regular issues such as large exposures. It is attended by a representative from Group Audit, as are the other main sector committees and any lower level committees we wish to attend. We add to the debates on particular issues and follow up on matters requiring audit involvement. If necessary, our plans are revised to take account of the changing risk profile of the group.

Other Group Control Functions

Group Audit is not the only internal body that helps management and the Board to meet their objectives. There are various other specialised functions that often have a more direct influence in the management of risks and often are deeply involved in specific areas on a daily basis. We take the view that these functions support management in controlling risks and, as with any other controls, we have the independent right to assess their effectiveness.

Other Banks

Although we are in competition with other High Street banks and building societies, there is considerable co-operation when it comes to the prevention of fraud, money laundering and breaches of security. We are represented on the British Bankers Association, which meets regularly to discuss topics of common interest and to give an united response to proposed changes to legislation or Bank of England regulations.

There are regular meetings between the heads of internal audit departments and specialist groups such as information systems auditors. There is also a regular liaison through meetings of the professional internal auditing and accounting bodies.

STANDARDS

Formal policies and standards are documented covering all aspects of our internal audit role, such as reporting lines, authorities, risk assessment, basic operating practices and professional behaviour.

Local internal audit functions within subsidiary companies are expected to comply with central policy but detailed standards may vary slightly to suit local corporate or legal requirements. Lord Justice Bingham was critical of the BCCI group of companies for its disparate structure and lack of central control and clearly it is important to maintain close links with our colleagues overseas. However, there is a conflict between this need for banks to have adequate central control in the country of the primary regulator and UK corporation tax legislation, which penalises a subsidiary company if it cannot demonstrate a sufficient degree of autonomy and independent control.

Independence

Independence allows us to plan and complete our work without undue influence or interference and enables auditors to render impartial, objective judgements. That is not to say that occasionally we will not slightly rearrange our plans to accommodate line management if there is no prejudice to the outcome of the audit.

Following the 1990 review, our place in the organisation is designed to ensure independence from line management, freedom of access to all group operations and direct input to the A&CC. The Board also ensures that the department is adequately funded to allow suitable coverage of the group's significant risks.

We try to ensure that audits are conducted in a way that allows auditors to have an honest belief in their work and that prevents significant quality compromises having to be made. Auditors are not placed in situations where there are potential conflicts of interest or where they feel unable to make objective professional judgements.

Audit reports and working papers are reviewed internally before a report is issued, ensuring that the work has been performed objectively as well as effectively.

Professional Proficiency

Group Audit management is responsible for ensuring that staff are technically proficient and suitably experienced to enable them to perform all identified audits. Staff are therefore encouraged to seek suitable professional auditing, computer auditing, banking or accounting qualifications.

In exercising due professional care, staff are expected to be alert to the possibility of intentional wrongdoing, fraud, errors, omissions, inefficiency and ineffectiveness. They are also expected to conduct themselves professionally and to avoid actions that might affect their objectivity or independence. They must notify senior management of any potential conflict of interest caused by an audit assignment.

Review and Quality Control

All Group Audit sections and subsidiary audit departments are responsible for reviewing the quality of their own audit work by the adoption of a continuous review process. Day to day supervision and review are undertaken by the lead auditor and a designated audit manager reviews the audit report, and associated papers, before the report is issued.

A separate quality control programme also ensures that policies, procedures and standards are consistently applied throughout the department. Staff from another section of Group Audit review a selection of files and the results are then used to develop and improve policies, standards and techniques. Working practices are continually reviewed to ensure that they remain relevant and appropriate to the changing operating environment within the group.

CONCLUSIONS

Group Audit

Following recommendations of the reporting accountants and the Bank of England in 1989, Group Audit began a major programme of change that has culminated in a far more professional, independent and effective internal audit function. We have the full support of the Board and our clearly defined role extends world-wide to cover all the group's operating risks and associated controls.

Our running costs may be significant but, while we remain professional and objective we provide a valuable service to management and the Board and fulfil an important role that helps to protect shareholders' investments. We report our major concerns independently to the non-executive members of the A&CC, and have regular meetings with our external auditors and the Bank of England.

Wider Implications

The Cadbury and Bingham reports recognised the importance of an effective internal audit function, but they did not elaborate on the ideal role, size or minimum standards of such a department. There are no statutory obligations on banks and UK companies in general to employ an internal audit function, and even the Bank of England's guidelines do not prescribe that all authorised institutions must have an internal audit function. It therefore becomes the responsibility of the A&CC, external auditors and reporting accountants to decide whether the absence or ineffectiveness of internal audit is detrimental to the internal control of the company. They would then be duty bound to advise the company's shareholders and to recommend suitable action by the Board.

Deciding what constitutes effective internal audit is primarily a question of judgement, but it has to be recognised that its role differs from, and is complementary to, that of the external auditors. The disparate sizes and activities of UK companies make it difficult to impose statutory minimum requirements, but the Standards and Guidelines of the Institute of Internal Auditors (UK) may provide a starting point. Perhaps directors or external auditors should be required to comment on performance against specific parameters, to allow shareholders to judge the quality and independence of the internal audit function.

The survival of a company depends more and more on the security and reliability of its operating systems, and internal audit plays an important role monitoring the controls over the development and use of these systems. The external auditors cannot be expected to review all the risks affecting a company on a daily basis and they have to rely to some degree on internal audit, which is closer to the operations of the business. It is not possible to anticipate every fraud or loss, but at least internal audit is able to respond immediately, where appropriate.

5

FINANCIAL CONTROL SYSTEMS IN THE NORTHERN BANK GROUP

John Trethowan
Manager, Strategic Planning,
Northern Bank Group

BACKGROUND

Northern Bank is a subsidiary of National Australia Bank Group, and the largest bank operating in Northern Ireland. Northern Bank's core activity is retail branch banking. In addition to delivering retail products, these branches are used as a delivery channel for the bank's Financial Services Division, and for treasury, leasing and factoring products.

EXTERNAL FINANCIAL CONTROLS

The main external elements which shape the bank's financial control systems are (a) Bank of England supervision; (b) parent bank activity; (c) IMRO/SIB supervision; and (d) external auditors.

Bank of England Supervision

The 1987 Banking Act gave the Bank of England powers of authorisation over internal systems and controls. These are outlined in the Bank's *Statement of Principles* (see Appendix 2) which were published shortly after the Act became law.

Under section 39 of the Banking Act, every bank must now satisfy the Bank of England that it maintains adequate accounting and other records, adequate systems and control, has non-executive directors, and satisfactory arrangements for internal and external audit.

Compliance is supervised by a meeting between the Bank of England's Review Team of bankers and accountants, and a senior team from Northern Bank Group (NBG). These meetings take place twice a year, in the spring and in the autumn. The meeting is not conducted to a prescribed model, but, rather, under the guidance of Supervisory Notes issued by the Bank of England.

The NBG delegation briefs the Review Team on all aspects of NBG's strategy and operations, as well as any specific business issue that may influence its financial position.

In addition, other issues, such as a commentary on the annual and interim financial results are given, together with an overview of the bank's liquidity, bad debt, and large exposure positions. The performance and compliance of the bank in completing mandatory Bank of England reports and returns is also discussed at this meeting.

The Review Team are also interested to hear NBG's opinion of the local economy, as this again is a key factor in the performance potential of the bank.

Parent Bank Activity

This is the other major external influence exerting financial control on the NBG. National Australia Bank Group, the parent, is a major transnational bank and, in addition to Northern Bank, has subsidiaries in Australia, New Zealand, the Republic of Ireland, and Yorkshire and Scotland in the UK.

The performance of all subsidiaries is actively managed at local level under the supervision of the parent holding company. The Group currently has a credit rating of AA3 with Moody's and AA with Standard and Poor's, and is conscious of the importance of the performance of each of its subsidiaries, in that analysts now look further than the group consolidated accounts when assessing performance.

Control of financial performance is achieved by the following:

1. Reporting systems. Financial reporting takes place monthly from all subsidiaries in a uniform format to aid analysis and consolidation.

   This takes the form of monthly profit and loss reporting against the monthly "milestone figures" on the NBG's annual operating plan. Additionally, at the end of each trading quarter a more in-depth analysis takes place when the bank's balance sheet volumes and earnings are examined and the variances to plan are analysed. As part of this process the year end position is re-forecast in the light of current trading conditions, so that remedial action can be targeted where necessary.

   The Chief Executive of NBG also regularly meets with his European subsidiary counterparts, under the auspices of National Australia Bank, to discuss each bank's performance and operating conditions.

2. Senior managers from the parent company are members of the Northern Bank Board.

3. NBG operationalises its performance objectives by specifying targets in key result areas. These embody a number of types of ratio and percentage comparative measures, which encompass all key areas of the Group's activities. The results form league table comparisons between the various Group members and also with industry leaders in each area of measurement. Again, this allows the parent to approach any subsidiary whose performance is below standard in any of the chosen areas.

IMRO/SIB Supervision

IMRO

Northern Bank is a member of IMRO, and Chapter V of the IMRO Rule Book contains the requirements for its members to maintain financial resources adequate for their business and to keep proper financial records.

These rules are applied under the "Lead Regulator" arrangements made between IMRO and the Bank of England in those banks where the investment business is comparatively small compared with its banking business. In these cases such banks are not subject to IMRO's financial rules. Instead, they are subject to the supervisory requirements by the Bank of England, under section 39 of the Banking Act.

In NBG, Chapter V IMRO rules are applied as follows:

	Application of Rules
Financial Resources Rules	
• Maintenance of financial resources	No
Accounting Records Rules	
• Maintenance of bank and customers' accounting records	Yes
• Submission of periodic financial returns	No
• Submission of Annual Accounts	Yes
Control and Systems Rules	
• Maintenance of internal controls	Yes
Ad Hoc Financial Notification Rules	
• Notices of breaches of the financial resources requirements	No
• Notice of audit qualification	Yes
Audit Rules	
• Arrangements, and content part of audit report relating to compliance with rules relating to customers' assets	Yes
• Client money regulations	Yes
• Contents of remainder of audit report	No

SIB

Northern Bank Insurance Services Ltd (NBIS), the bank's financial services arm, is regulated in investment business by the Securities and Investment Board (SIB). Chapter II, part 3, of the SIB rules sets out the requirement for a low-risk firm as follows:

1. A low-risk firm shall have and maintain in respect of its investment business such financial resources that will ensure that the firm is, at all times, able to meet its liabilities as they fall due.

2. In so doing, the firm may use any such assets which are available to meet any of its liabilities.

To show that these requirements have been satisfied, NBIS Ltd completes an annual declaration and submits audited accounts to the Securities and Investment Board.[1]

External Auditors

Under the Companies Act the bank's auditors are required to report whether:

1. The accounts have been prepared in accordance with the requirements of the Act.

2. The accounts give a true and fair view of the state of the bank's affairs and of its profit or loss for the year.

If the external auditors decide to qualify their audit opinion they must immediately notify the Bank of England. The auditors have a statutory right of access to the bank's accounting records, and to all information and explanations considered necessary for the audit.

The bank's auditors work very closely with the bank's internal audit department in planning the scope, nature and extent of their internal work each year. The aim is to ensure coverage of the areas perceived as being of highest risk to the bank, and to avoid unnecessary and costly duplication of effort in less critical areas.

On conclusion of their audit each year, the auditors produce a management letter in which they make comment on specific

---

[1] With effect from 9 January 1995, NBIS Ltd is regulated by the Personal Investment Authority. In consequence, SIB formally withdrew authorisation on 25 January 1995.

issues which they have identified in the bank's systems of internal control or accounting procedures, and suggest improvements for the bank to consider implementing. This management letter is regarded as very important by both the bank and the auditors.

INTERNAL FINANCIAL CONTROLS

The Internal Financial Controls encompassed within the NBG are (a) Board of Directors (including the Audit Committee); (b) Finance Department; (c) Audit and Security Department; (d) Compliance Department; (e) Asset and Liability Committee; and (f) Credit Bureau.

Board of Directors

The Northern Bank Board meets monthly and consists of a mixture of representatives from the parent holding company, executive directors and non-executive directors. The Board overviews the operation of the bank, and receives regular reports on its financial performance, and on credit and large exposure issues. There are also less frequent reports on other strategic and operational issues.

Together with the parent holding company, the Board also approves changes to the bank's Management Operating Delegations. This is a formalised system whereby each tier of management has its level of authority quantified in the areas in which they operate (for example, how much they can lend without further approval).

Members of the Board also sit on the bank's Audit Committee. This committee consists of three non-executive directors, who meet at least three times a year with the Chief Executive in attendance. Representatives of the external auditors and the bank's internal audit and finance functions are also in attendance at most meetings.

The duties of the Audit Committee are:

1. To maintain open lines of communication among the Board, the external auditors, Internal Audit and company management to exchange information and views.

2. To oversee and appraise the independence, quality, cost-effectiveness and extent of the total audit effort.

3. To perform an independent overview of the financial information prepared by the bank's management for external parties.

4. To determine the adequacy and effectiveness of the bank's internal control systems and evaluate the operation thereof.

Finance Department

As might be expected, the bank's Finance Department executes a pivotal role in managing systems of internal financial control. As already described under parent bank activity there is a major input to the main management accounting reporting channels. It also bears responsibility for a number of other key areas of internal financial control, as follows:

1. As a member of the United Kingdom "banking sector", NBG is subject to supervision by the Bank of England and this demands production of voluminous statistical data, which must be both accurate and available within rigid reporting deadlines.

2. NBG is subject to United Kingdom Companies Act legislation, one element of which is the production of audited financial statements.

3. Compliance with miscellaneous taxation legislation affects the bank in a variety of ways and the Finance Department is responsible for development of policy in response to the demands of such legislation. Corporation tax computation is a significant area and, as a member of a global banking group, taxation considerations can be very wide-ranging in their scope. To maximise taxation efficiency and effectiveness, close liaison is maintained with the parent bank which has a specialist tax team available for consultative purposes.

4. NBG tends towards a centralised philosophy in the finance sphere as this is regarded as the most cost effective and ef-

ficient mode of operation. This extends to the production of principal management accounting reporting for the segmented business units including retail, corporate, treasury and international functions. In the case of the largest business unit, the retail network, management accounts are available for individual branches as well as any consolidated permutation. Centralised systems include general ledger, fixed assets, accounts payable and capital expenditure appraisal.

5. The planning function of the bank is also domiciled in the Finance Department, given the significance of the financial components in the formalised plan documentation. This is particularly the case for short term periods of up to one year, when very detailed financial profiles are produced which are subject to formalised review of actual performance against plan on a quarterly basis. In order to support this degree of financial supervision and analysis, extensive investment has taken place in the development of advanced micro-based computer systems.

6. Given the diversity and complexity of the financial profile of NBG, members of the management team are represented on senior committees as follows:

   • Asset and Liability Committee — responsible for optimising the bank's earnings through management of the structural interest rate risk inherent in the balance sheet.

   • Interest Rate Committee — responsible for ratification of pricing decisions in response to competitive considerations or general movements in United Kingdom interest rates.

   • Product Performance Review Committee — responsible for periodic review of balance sheet volume performance and corresponding pricing issues.

   • Costing Committee — responsible for fees and tariffs on all banking services.

- Strategic Project Assessment Committee — responsible for assessing capital and non-recurring revenue expenditure proposals within a value-based management framework.

Audit and Security Department

In common with the rest of the banking industry, NBG's audit function has undergone a material change in its role over the past ten years or so. To a large extent this has been due to the significant diversification that has taken place as the bank has entered new markets such as mortgages and financial services. Its original supervisory role could be regarded as a form of policing. But the diversity that has now taken place has created a sense of partnership where audit subjects now perceive the once dreaded exercise as a positive and constructive way of creating a better organisation.

While it is true to say that the controls exercised by Audit do not deal specifically with issues of a financial nature there is, nonetheless, an important degree of supervision and control implicit in their work. They have, therefore, a direct line of responsibility to the Board and Chief Executive which ensures objectivity is achieved.

Audit is divided into a number of areas as follows:

Traditional Branch Audit

This is the simplest area of control, though the subject is extensive given the scope of activities and the size of the branch network. Branch operations tend towards very consistent procedural parameters and the audit team are able to use micro-based systems to assist in their audit sampling, analysis and report production.

The major thrust of Branch Audit is conformity with procedural controls, but it is anticipated that a further major change in the perspective of control will occur as the NBG becomes a more customer-focused sales and marketing organisation. This is particularly important, as employees increasingly perceive their roles changing and the axiom of administrative excellence above all else begins to diminish. Clearly, for such a cultural change to occur successfully the audit function must change in tandem with it.

Head Office Audit

This is a fairly recent segmentation of internal systems of control and, again, its emergence has arisen from the extensive expansion of the bank's services including the development of specialist subsidiaries in areas such as financial services, leasing and factoring.

In contrast to the more orderly nature of Branch Audit it is necessary to develop differentiated risk profiles of various Head Office functions to ensure that the frequency and depth of audit is commensurate with the perceived risk.

Computer Audit

As the bank's investment in, and reliance on, information technology has increased there has been a corresponding need to ensure that effective systems of control are in place to minimise this area of material risk.

A dedicated team of specialists deal with such areas as central and network systems, methodology for software research and development, customer-activated devices and networks, computer standards and support to external audit.

The audit function is also responsible for policy on physical security.

Compliance Department

As the bank's business operations have diversified and the degree of statutory and self-regulation has expanded, so it has been necessary to create a supervisory body to ensure that such controls are observed.

Compliance Department acts as a "sounding board" for the organisation to advise on what is often a jargon-ridden technical area. Two of NBG's financial services subsidiaries are regulated by SIB and IMRO, and both have an in-house compliance unit to ensure that these highly specialised and technically complex areas are supervised correctly.

In addition to acting as an advisory unit in a large range of compliance issues associated with the Financial Services Act, the Compliance Department also undertakes management of the following areas:

1. The bank is licensed to conduct consumer credit business under the Consumer Credit Act. This implies observance of a very strict code with substantial complexity in administration and documentation.

2. The Data Protection Act, which deals with computerised information on customers and the proper and lawful management of such data, including its unauthorised use or disclosure.

3. The Code of Banking Practice is a voluntary form of regulation but one that is taken very seriously in an effort to ensure that the bank is perceived to be at the forefront of maintaining a high standard of corporate and business ethics.

4. The Compliance Department also reviews new product development, including associated advertising material.

Asset and Liability Committee

The function of the Asset and Liability Committee (ALCO) is to optimise net interest income earnings by the active management of the structural interest rate risk inherent in the balance sheet, with a view to eliminating major areas of risk.

Interest rate risk arises from differences or mismatches in the timing of changes and/or the resetting of interest rates on the bank's fixed term sterling and currency assets and liabilities, including off-balance sheet instruments.

The Asset and Liability Committee is chaired by the Chief Executive and includes senior management from Treasury, Marketing, Planning and Finance. It meets at least monthly or more frequently during periods of interest rate volatility where short term responses are essential.

Whilst the bank has developed high quality systems for "most likely" financial outcomes, it has been necessary to employ custom-designed simulation software to support the ALCO process.

The simulation model contains a complete price and maturity profile of the bank's balance sheet in a very detailed format. It is possible to develop several scenarios simultaneously and to judge their effect on the bank's net interest income earnings. ALCO will consider the various options, and policy directives will be issued and operationally implemented by the bank's Treasury Division.

ALCO is also responsible for ensuring conformance with policy directives on liquidity management.

Credit Bureau

The Credit Bureau is the principal unit within NBG responsible for controlling policy on lending and, in particular, management of credit risk and prudential risk.

As a subsidiary, NBG has adopted the credit culture of its Australian parent in relation to, for example, hierarchical controls, accounting policies in areas such as bad debts and non-performing loans and systems for assessing the relative quality of the asset portfolio.

Lending is essentially concerned with the observation of fundamental principles and the process is controlled by the use of sanction and overview levels ranging from individual account managers in the retail network to the Board of the parent company.

Miscellaneous internal reporting is conducted on a regular basis for lending where the credit risk is considered to be high, for example, irregular accounts, potential problem loans, restructured loans, non-accrual loans etc.

In addition to consideration of asset quality issues, the Credit Bureau is also charged with responsibility for the development of effective risk/reward pricing systems. The attainment of such goals is an integral part of the external performance assessment by the parent. The primary measures of asset quality are the net specific bad debt charge and the level of non-accrual loans as a percentage of risk-weighted assets.

6

DEVELOPMENT OF ORGANISATIONAL RISK CONTROL SYSTEMS

Cyril Bennett

Senior Manager, Treasury Risk Control,
AIB Group Treasury

INTRODUCTION

The control of risk in financial institutions — its associated costs and benefits — should be considered in the context of the market volatility and uncertainty experienced over the last five years. In this period, the extent of uncertainty in the financial markets has been extraordinary and its impact unrelenting. From the stock market crash of 1987 to the effective suspension of the ERM in August 1993, the international financial system has been in a state of continuous stress. In the intervening period the system has been subject to a variety of global and local disruptions. These included the US Savings and Loans credit default, the Local Authority Swap *ultra vires* rulings, the Drexel Burnham Lambert Chapter 11 filing, the Iraqi invasion of Kuwait and the subsequent Gulf war, the financial collapse of the Bank of New England, instability in the global real estate/property sector, and, of course, BCCI. This period of unprecedented transition and uncertainty, which has reinforced the need for effective internal controls, seems set to continue.

No single risk management approach or commercial philosophy will insulate a financial institution from the effects of unexpected events on an ongoing basis. However, good management practice and appropriate business focused controls are likely to afford long-term protection to an organisation.

Furthermore, they are the essential core values/mechanisms required to facilitate commercial risk-taking in the context of uncertain markets. They can help to ensure a long-term ability to maintain a profitable presence in chosen markets.

Allied to the general increased uncertainty in the markets is the development of significant industry change. The emergence of greater regulation, the elevation in importance of shareholder value and board governance, increased competition as a consequence of deregulation and the development of the Single European Market have all contributed to a clearer stratification of market participants. Greater focus on credit quality in the context of volatile, and often illiquid, markets has increased competitive pressure for several organisations. In addition, the cost of remaining competitive in the technology race, and the challenges forced on management in tackling their cost bases, have altered the dynamics of the financial market.

Within this more competitive environment stratification is not applied solely to credit status — it extends to differentiation between the technically sophisticated and the unsophisticated, between the cost-efficient and the inefficient, between the risk-focused and the unfocused. In such circumstances unwanted and excessive risk ends with the weakest, unfocused and less sophisticated participants in the market, with predictable consequences.

Accordingly, bank management need to be ever more vigilant: to be fully informed of the risks being taken and ensure that the organisation has adequate defence mechanisms to manage these risks.

Against this background, the issue of building a control framework to insulate the organisation from unwarranted risk emerges as a critical winning strategy for the next decade. An analysis of historic "crisis" events and an understanding of their devastating impact on individual organisations can assist management in the development of appropriate responses to the increasing uncertainty in the market.

DEVELOPMENT OF AN ORGANISATIONAL RISK CONTROL SYSTEM

Building greater protection for the long term against unanticipated risk can be considered in the context of either (a) the internal organisation response or (b) industry response.

This chapter is primarily concerned with the internal organisation response. It is written largely in the context of a capital markets banking operation. Nonetheless, many of the principles and procedures outlined have a universal application across any type of financial organisation. As such, it attempts to identify some of the key issues for consideration in relation to the proactive management of risk.

All financial organisations accept and manage risk on an ongoing basis. A central objective for every financial institution should be to develop, on the one hand, resilience against unanticipated events and, on the other, sufficient expertise and confidence to exploit profitably opportunities arising from volatility and uncertain markets, within acceptable risk parameters. Ongoing success in getting the balance right is a function of a number of initiatives specific to each institution. The development of appropriate defence mechanisms within an organisation is of pivotal importance. It involves, amongst other things, the development of an all-pervasive management philosophy. In certain organisations where the current management approach is weak, the development of such a philosophy is a longer-term project.

Some of the critical attributes of institutions that manage risk successfully are:

- Leadership

- Identifiable risk culture

- Appropriate organisation structure

- Business responsive policy framework

- Risk review/Control process.

Leadership

In any organisation and particularly those involved in the management of risk, the issue of leadership is critically important. Leadership in terms of risk management manifests itself internally within the organisation in terms of:

- Clarity of purpose

- An appreciation of the dynamics of the business

- An acceptance of the concept that risk taking is central to generating and growing profitable business

- A recognition and appreciation of the dangers of risk concentration and the benefits of risk diversification

- The courage to avoid the "herd instinct", which often drives developments in the markets.

Given these attributes, the issue of leadership seamlessly evolves into the development and articulation of a risk culture. An objective analysis of successful organisations would indicate that the greater the success of the organisation, the more defined and ingrained is the risk culture.

Identifiable Risk Culture

Three dimensions exist in relation to an organisation's risk culture: (a) definition, (b) communication, and (c) visibility.

Definition

An organisation's risk culture encompasses a number of factors, including:

- The degree to which the organisation recognises the value of liquidity as an overall protection mechanism to absorb any adverse impact on the organisation of unanticipated events

- The identification of risks that the individual organisation wishes to avoid at all costs

- The identification of unavoidable risks and the establishment of appropriate management responses

- The identification of risks that the organisation is willing to embrace, within appropriate prudential limits, and the subsequent management of these risks with the objective of adequately remunerating shareholders' funds.

Communication

Communication of the risk culture is dependent upon both formal and informal channels. Evidence of management practices which demonstrate a clear and sharp focus on risk is the single most significant means of communicating and ensuring the assimilation of the risk culture into the organisation at all levels.

Other techniques that supplement such senior management practices include:

- Integration of the risk culture concept into all in-house training programmes

- Senior management participation in the risk profile review process

- Formal existence of risk procedures and policy manuals

- The existence within the organisation of a board/senior management risk limit approval process

- Incentivised management processes which focus on the management of risk and the overall return generated.

Visibility

The process of *making risk visible* in the organisation is closely aligned to the communication process. The review of the risk profile by senior management with a comprehensive questioning approach heightens the visibility of risk. The development of a consistent basis for the identification and quantification of risk across all activities allows a meaningful comparison of businesses by reference to the quantum of risk undertaken. This further heightens the awareness at all levels in the organisation of the risk profile.

Many organisations in recent years have introduced a formalised process which requires competing units within a business to apply for capacity and justify on an ongoing basis its stewardship of resources allocated. The most meaningful universal risk language is the underlying capital of the organisation. All competing activities within a business should be reviewed in the context of the return that is generated with respect to the "capital at risk". The development of such risk-related performance measurement mechanisms is a powerful tool for raising the visibility and proactive management of risk.

The use of "capital at risk" as the universal risk language within an organisation implies that many of the formalised limit control mechanisms established will be expressed in this form. In this context, successful "risk visibility" manifests itself in all business generators being aware of the quantum of risk (capital at risk) they are managing and the potential return on that risk.

Appropriate Organisation Structure

Given the existence of an appropriate risk culture, the next stage in the process of ensuring adequate protection against the adverse consequence of uncertainty is to ensure that appropriate organisational structures exist. In this regard the organisational options need to be considered in the context of the following functions: (a) business generation, (b) policy development, and (c) review/control.

Business Generation Functions

As a guiding principle, the organisational design should fully complement the strategy of the organisation. In the context of managing risk, this implies that the successful companies develop business strategies and structures around their core risk competencies and management skills.

A related issue concerns the degree of delegation and authority in relation to business generation or the management of risk positions. As a general principle it is accepted that the authority for decision-making should rest as close to the market interface as possible. However, this high degree of autonomy needs to be balanced with an aggressive review process at the more senior management levels of the business division.

Policy Development Functions

The optimum organisational structure for the formulation of business-focused policy is represented by a network approach. Initially the process should involve a combination of business originators, risk control accounting and information system specialists. It is essential that risk policies should be driven by prudent business opportunities, needs and objectives. Independent approval by an appropriate senior management forum is essential. Increasingly, regulators and rating agencies look for evidence of formal policies and examine the policy formulation process in the course of institutional assessment.

A responsive approval process system is often essential in the case of innovative risk activities, products or structures. This can result in tension between the business generation function, which may be in a competitive situation, and the approval process, which demands a more detailed and rigorous assessment of new activities. Senior management must be aware and responsive to these competing needs.

Risk Review Functions

The general industry model for the review and control of risk positions usually takes place through the creation and resourcing of a separate independent function. However, within some organisations the risk review and control process is significantly more refined, with review taking place at several different levels:

- Dealer level
- Desk level
- Dealing room level
- Group Treasury Level
- Asset and Liability Committee
- Main Board.

In a multilocation environment, the head of each trading room is fully responsible for ensuring adherence to all allocated risk limits.

The responsibility of the risk monitoring unit is to ensure the independent identification of all risks, their classification and quantification. Once these three stages have been completed, scenario testing, against worst-case expectations, identifies the magnitude of the risk against approved limits and the organisation's risk appetite.

Business-responsive Policy Framework

The fourth stage in the development of a risk-resilient organisation is centred on the issue of the development of business-focused policy.

Key attributes of good policy are:

- Joint development of policy with business generators and control functions

- Policy formulation consistency with the business and financial objectives of the institution

- Clarity in regard to the identification and definition of risk covered by the policy

- Identification of the scope of the policy, for example, risks that are excluded from the policy etc.

- Identification of the capital at risk limit proposed for this activity

- Identification of the revenue potential arising from the planned activity and the determination of the target return on capital used to sustain the proposed business activity

- Clarity with regard to the specification of management responsibility for monitoring and control of the risk under management

- Harmonious policy and information technology strategies.

Risk Review/Control Process

Within any organisation risk manifests itself in many guises. Initially we generally consider as priority risks those that relate to financial transactions, assets or customers. However, *non*-financial risks can have an equally disruptive impact on revenue and overall operational ability. Some of the key risks that need to be addressed to ensure ongoing successful risk management are outlined in Figure 1 on the following page.

RISK CONTROL: MANAGEMENT VS REGULATORY NEEDS

Increased regulation over recent years has resulted in increased focus on the allocation of capital to support credit risk. Recent initiatives from the Bank of International Settlements, the European Community and the US Federal Reserve all propose to extend the allocation of capital to cover market risk. This raises the question of the needs of regulators versus the needs of management, and whether regulation imposes an unnecessary and heavy cost on financial institutions. Published data in the United States have suggested that regulation imposes a heavy cost on the industry. Whether or not one accepts this premise, the following points are of relevance in assessing the net cost of regulation on the industry, that is, regulator-imposed requirements relative to prudent management practices.

Managements of successful organisations invariably impose constraints on their activities. In many circumstances, prudent management constraints address the same issues as regulators. However, often the standardised approach of regulators requires significant duplication of effort.

Figure 1: Risks and Control Processes

Risk	Possible Control Process
Liquidity funding	• Policy constraints on quality, concentration and term of assets and liabilities • Diversified sources • Maintenance of capital adequacy ratios • Maintenance of high international credit rating • Tested liquidity contingency plan
Foreign exchange rate	• Formal limits expressed in capital at risk
Interest rate equity underwriting	• Equivalents or limits on nominal net open positions
Credit	• Individual counterparty limits
Settlement	• Individual counterparty limits
Clearing	• Individual counterparty limits
Product/Transaction	• Rigorous worst-case scenario testing for inclusion in macro market/credit risk limits or specific product limits
Sector concentration	• Sector limits
Large exposures	• Maximum exposure limits
Systems	• Rigorous testing and maintenance. • Back up contingency plan. • Ongoing investment
Legal	• Documentation/Legal securities unit
Key personnel	• Competitive remuneration packages • Rewarding environment

The significant costs associated with regulation arise where supervisory requirements lack consistency across products/ activities. Of particular importance in this regard are certain inconsistencies that exist with the Bank of International Settlements' Capital Adequacy standards. In this regard, it is questionable if the standards are sufficiently finely tuned to assist management and, accordingly, result in the imposition of unnecessary costs. Specific examples include:

- The inadequacy of credit differentiation in international standards

- Excessive credit risk assessment for derivative activities

- Differences between international initiatives concerning regulators' proposals for the provisioning of capital to cover market risk.

In each case certain international banks will be disadvantaged and suffer an unnecessary cost relative to their peers.

Finally, in the case of Irish banks, supervisory requirements in relation to the maintenance of liquidity are excessive relative to either management's prudential requirements or international standards. Such distortions impose a heavy cost on financial institutions, their customer base and the economy as a whole.

More generally, significant costs are imposed by regulation as a direct consequence of unfocused and inconsistent regulation. This distorts the true economics of business and can lead to uncommercial decisions, or inappropriate concentration of risk, in the longer term.

SUMMARY

This chapter outlined the fundamental elements involved in establishing a framework for protecting a bank against the inevitable uncertainties inherent in present and prospective business environment. The critical issues for institutions that wish to develop a risk control philosophy to manage overall performance successfully over the longer term are:

- Strong leadership

- Visible and living risk culture

- Appropriate organisation structure

- Business responsive policy framework

- Independent risk review/control process.

With this framework in place organisations should be better able to weather the effects of uncertainty and capitalise on opportunities in the business environment.

7

THE EXTERNAL AUDITOR/ REPORTING ACCOUNTANT PERSPECTIVE

Steve Almond
Group Partner, Touche Ross

THE NEED FOR EFFECTIVE INTERNAL CONTROLS IN BANKING

Informed opinion is agreed: banking is an increasingly complex business. The Banking Act definition of a bank as an institution which is carrying on a deposit taking business does not even begin to tell the story of the UK banking scene in the 1990s, where over 400 banks are competing with each other and with other financial institutions across a wide range of financial services, and actually only a very small proportion are in the High Street pitching for the current and savings account business of the average member of the public. More than ever, banking is a risk business, with many thousands of multi-million pound risk decisions being taken every single day. Daily risks faced by bank management include:

- Not being repaid by a borrower (credit risk)
- Running out of cash (liquidity risk)
- Getting it wrong in the dealing room (position risk)
- Losing control (operational risk)
- Being deceived by an employee or a customer (fraud).

Whilst credit risk is still, perhaps, the one most feared by bankers, position risk has undoubtedly become more important as banks have expanded their dealing and risk management services. Any of the above risk types can bring a bank to its knees. The need for an effective system of internal control is therefore paramount.

Why is banking any different from other industry sectors? A quick look at any bank's balance sheet provides part of the answer to this. Almost all balance sheet items are derived in some way or another from movements of cash, and as banks are typically much more highly geared than other businesses, the origin of most of that cash is depositors' back pockets. Company directors are typically regarded as being responsible for the stewardship of a company's assets, and thereby the interests of the shareholders. This is equally true of bank directors, but they must also have regard to the interests of the depositors.

The other part of the answer is that the UK banks, taken together, comprise the UK banking system and it is essential to have public confidence in that system.

These public interest factors also cause the banks to be subject to a significantly higher degree of independent examination than other business sectors. Prior to the emergence of corporate governance as a popular issue, corporate UK has had precious little exposure beyond the statutory audit to independent scrutiny or measurement against standards of best practice. It is not surprising, therefore, that internal control has been one of the thorniest issues for the Cadbury Committee. As a regulated industry, on the other hand, the banks are well used to baring their souls to third parties, and having themselves measured against their competitors. By and large, the Cadbury Committee is just adding another layer, as is the establishment of the banking ombudsman.

This is not necessarily to say that internal controls in banks are that much more effective than elsewhere in corporate UK, but the demands for well developed internal controls are that much greater.

WHAT MAKES AN INTERNAL CONTROL ENVIRONMENT EFFECTIVE?

In its paper BSD/1987/2, the Bank of England provided, as guidance, lists of things that might be important in a typical bank's reporting and control systems. In the recently released revised version of this paper (BSD/1994/2), these lists have been dropped. Why? Perhaps it was felt to be unwise to be over-prescriptive in what is a highly judgmental area. This could encourage a bank to regard itself as perfect if it were able to tick off all the items in a rather mechanistic fashion. Equally, any critic of a bank could charge it with being deficient if it did not score 100 per cent on the checklist, regardless of how limited its scope of activities might be.

So what is best practice? What constitutes an effective internal control environment? Easy to ask, difficult to answer. It doesn't matter how detailed or precise a system of internal controls is, if a bank's management lacks integrity or professional skill and judgement. This is precisely why these attributes feature in the minimum standards for banking authorisation embodied in Schedule 3 to the Banking Act, 1987. The reverse is, of course, also true, which is why Schedule 3 also calls for adequate records and controls.

It is the effectiveness of the exercise of internal controls in practice that really counts, not their apparent merits according to any text book. Clearly, when a bank collapses it is revealing to look at what went wrong and to learn the control lessons for the future. But it is a bit late at that stage. It is much harder — much less obvious from the outside — to attribute a bank's continued good health to the strength of particular controls.

One good test of effectiveness is to consider management's reaction to a breach of an established control procedure. For instance, what is the reaction to a trader exceeding his position limit or to the back office falling behind with certain account reconciliations? If such dealer excesses are routinely signed off, or no remedial action is taken to clear the reconciliation backlog, bank management should not be surprised if, sooner or later, they face unexpected trading losses or a deluge of complaints and claims from correspondent banks. A rapid and effective response to a control problem, on the other hand, suggests a tightly observed control environment, and demonstrates to staff that management expect it to continue that way.

Another useful question to ask is what the impact would be if a particular control were withdrawn. In some institutions, the control structure may comprise many layers of routine checks and double checks carried out for the large part by relatively junior or inexperienced members of staff. But where the command hierarchy and the tradition of managerial authority is at that level, the internal control structure can be blown over like so many matchsticks by a determined and forceful senior official. If a control procedure can be safely withdrawn, then, for efficiency and clarity, it is better to do so. Emphasis can then be placed on those key controls that really matter, and ensuring that they are operated and supervised by staff and management with the appropriate training and experience.

It is also interesting to question why a particular system-level control seems to operate better in some environments than in others. The answer seems to lie in the differences in corporate cultures. Some banks seem to thrive on a structure of committees and decision by consensus, whereas others work better with clearly delegated decision making powers to the individual, reflecting his position and his experience. Some rely upon detailed re-performance and independent checking on a transaction by transaction basis; others focus much more on reporting of exceptions only. Strictly defined job descriptions and delineation of duties are essential in certain corporate cultures, but might prove suffocating in others with flatter hierarchies and a tradition of team-working.

It is important, therefore, to ensure that the internal control environment is compatible with the bank's corporate culture. This is particularly pertinent when talking about "best practice". The UK banking industry has a wealth of external advice available to it — from the supervisor, the internal auditor, the external auditor, consultants, and its own associations such as the British Bankers Association and the London Investment

Banking Association. It is essential, however, that bank management and advisers alike recognise and remember that the UK banking industry comprises a wide range of institutions, both in the scope and the scale of their activities, and what is good control practice for one simply may not work for another. Of course, there should be many common features and the work of these parties should help to ensure that a reasonably high minimum standard is established and maintained. The overriding conclusion, however, is that it is the effectiveness, not the simple existence, of controls that counts. And even effective controls will still not prevent a bank (or indeed any other business) from losing lots of money because of poor judgement, lack of integrity or unforeseen macroeconomic problems.

THE COST OF CONTROL: A BARRIER TO ENTRY?

The comfortable notion of the High Street bank manager as the pillar of his community, manager of the local economy, and trusted custodian of the people's savings, has gone forever. Today's banking environment is typified by:

- High volume trading activity

- Sophisticated cross-market position taking

- Global 24-hour markets

- Complex relationships with major corporate customers

- Branches becoming sales offices, selling many different products

- An increasingly demanding regulatory environment

- Increasingly sophisticated fraudsters and money launderers

- A legal minefield in dealing with customers, enforcing security, and avoiding director-type responsibility.

The demands of all this on the control environment are severe. Increasingly, it is simply not possible to rely upon labour intensive manual procedures, underpinned by the routine inspection department checking for compliance with procedures manuals. Traditionally, the City has been prepared to invest millions in recruiting top quality front-office personnel, and housing them in high-tech dealing rooms. The better banks are now also recognising the need to make similar investments in their control environments, providing increasingly automated and sophisticated control tools, and putting highly skilled, highly paid people into key support positions. The emergence of the "middle office" in many of the more sophisticated trading houses is evidence of this.

Similarly, in the credit business, technological solutions are increasingly being applied to the demands of managing the relationships and associated risks with complex multinational corporate customers. Sophisticated information systems are required to provide the loan officer with an accurate and timely picture of the bank's aggregated credit exposure to a particular customer across all its financial activities and in all of its geographic locations. To counter the credit risk minefield of doing business with such customers, some banks have promoted the function of the "back office credit guru" to the point where he is a greater challenge than the external competition for the marketing loan officer seeking to write new business.

Commentators in recent years have often observed that the banking sector has outgrown itself, and that with too many banks chasing too little business the industry will shrink. Whilst this may have some truth in it, there is perhaps another side to the story. That is, that the need for very heavy investment in automated systems and high quality people to establish and maintain the necessary standard of internal control systems to keep pace with an increasingly complex and risky business environment is, in itself, a barrier to entry for new players — or, perhaps more relevant, to the expansion of smaller banks, which in due course will fall prey to their bigger brethren.

THE EXTERNAL AUDITOR AND
THE REPORTING ACCOUNTANT

Much has been said about the work and the responsibilities of the external auditor and the reporting accountant. It is important to distinguish between their roles. The external auditor's focus is on the truth and fairness of a bank's annual statutory financial statements. His work is designed to enable him to form an opinion thereon; he does not seek to deliver an opinion on the internal control systems. He should be interested in internal controls, but only in so far as they are relevant to the financial statements, and he will test the operation of such controls only to the extent that he intends to rely upon them in forming his opinion on the financial statements.

Auditing is a very competitive business in the UK today, and fee pressures mean that the auditor will do the minimum and most cost-effective work necessary to support his opinion. Whilst the *Auditing Guideline — Banks in the United Kingdom* states that the external auditor will normally need to place some reliance on internal control, it was written largely with the major banks in mind, whose range of activities and large branch networks make it unlikely that the auditor could undertake sufficient substantive verification of transactions on a cost effective basis.

As mentioned earlier, however, the UK banking sector encompasses a wide range of institutions, and, in many cases, a cost effective audit approach will involve a heavy emphasis on substantive verification of transactions and balances, rather than detailed testing of controls.

The approach of the reporting accountant, on the other hand, is almost the opposite. The reporting accountant is appointed by his client, at the behest of the Bank of England under section 39 of the Banking Act, 1987. His principal task is to examine, in accordance with the scope set by the Bank of England each year, the accounting and other records and internal control systems of the bank that have been established and maintained during the period under review, and to report exceptions to the guidelines set out in the Bank of England's paper, BSD/1994/2.

Within the scope set, therefore, the reporting accountant is concerned with the existence and maintenance of records and controls over the operation of the business, without focusing on any particular financial statements or other sets of results.

It is worth noting that neither the external auditor nor the reporting accountant is directly concerned about whether the bank has made a profit or a loss, whether it could have made a bigger profit (or a smaller loss), or how it has performed compared to its competitors. The auditor is concerned to see that the financial impact of the business operations during the period has been properly reflected in the financial statements. The reporting accountant's concern is whether an effective system of recording and controlling those business operations has been maintained throughout the period.

Clearly, in order to provide a valued service to clients, both the auditor and the reporting accountant will be keen to advise banking clients on the scope for profit improvement and control efficiency, but this would not be done as part of the formal reporting duties.

Notwithstanding these limitations on their formal duties, the business of the external auditor and the reporting accountant is increasingly risky. Oft-quoted factors include:

- The expectation gap, where a variety of third parties assume a bank's internal control systems must be sound simply because they are subject to external audit

- A more litigious environment, where the auditor's professional indemnity insurance often makes him a more attractive target than the directors of a collapsed client

- Exposure of banks' systems to examinations by other parties, such as Bank of England "review teams" or the SFA's Enforcement Division

- Increasing focus on fraud and money laundering

- The statutory duty to report to the regulators.

The last is worth a further comment. As mentioned earlier, internal controls are unlikely to be proof against management that is lacking in either integrity or professional skill, and a soundly controlled banking business can still lose lots of money if poor risk decisions are made. The duty to report has been introduced by statutory instrument, in the aftermath of BCCI, and it is effective for banks in the United Kingdom from 1 May 1994. It adds to, rather than replaces, the right to report which is embodied in section 47 of the Banking Act.

The statutory duty arises when the auditor or reporting accountant, in the ordinary course of his work as such, becomes aware of a matter that gives him reasonable cause to believe that the institution may be in breach of any of the Schedule 3 criteria, and thus is likely to be of material significance for the exercise of any of the Bank's functions under the Act. Although there is no requirement for the auditor or reporting accountant to seek out grounds for reporting, the imposition of the duty is nevertheless a weighty increase to his responsibilities. He must be much more mindful of the Schedule 3 criteria than hitherto, particularly perhaps of those aspects of the criteria which go beyond financial soundness, such as the requirements for directors and others to be "fit and proper persons" and for the business to be carried on with integrity and professional skill.

He must also generally be more sensitive to the Bank of England's point of view as supervisor in order to assess whether any actual or potential breach he comes across is likely to be of material significance. Lastly, the statutory duty, by increasing auditors' responsibilities to the Bank of England, may make it more difficult for the auditor to enjoy the same degree of openness in his professional relationship with his client.

HOW SHOULD THE AUDITOR/ REPORTING ACCOUNTANT RESPOND?

Good auditing and accounting skills are unlikely, in themselves, to be enough when dealing with complex banking institutions. The expectation of client and regulator alike for a greater knowledge of the bank's business means that the team of the auditor or reporting accountant need:

- Specialist experience

- More senior level involvement

- The support of specialist training and technical back-up

- To be in touch with the market place

- To have a knowledge of relevant legislation and regulation

- To be aware of emerging banking issues.

Without these factors, at the very least, the service is likely to lead to client dissatisfaction, whilst, at worst, it could lead to unwanted calls on the professional indemnity insurance policy.

8

INTERNAL BANK CONTROLS: AN AGENDA FOR DIALOGUE

Ray Kinsella

This concluding chapter highlights some of the more important issues relating to the development of internal controls systems in banks and their impact on the operational efficiency, stability and cost structures of banks. It would be presumptuous at this stage to seek to resolve these issues. An intensive debate, based on more research, including an analysis of the experience of the main participants within the existing framework, is needed.

THE KEY ROLE OF INTERNAL CONTROLS

Internal controls are central to the financial integrity of an individual bank and, equally, to the stability of the wider set of financial markets of which they are the basic unit. It has already been pointed out that banks are, perhaps uniquely, vulnerable to the impact of fraud and the subversion of controls. This has, of course, always been the case. What has changed — as the preceding contributions demonstrate — is the *environment* within which banks now operate — an environment which magnifies the scope for, and potential impact of, a failure of internal controls.

Technology — encompassing, as Walsh notes, information systems and advanced computerised systems — has created an integrated global marketplace in which shocks are easily transmitted across markets. Deregulation has heightened this effect. Highly sophisticated software, building on developments in finance theory, has created the capacity to "unbundle" and transpose risk across increasingly integrated financial institutions and markets. This has created a concomitant need — not yet met — for on-line monitoring and control systems, accessible to management, as a central element in a bank's internal control process.

Equally, banks themselves, driven by these pressures, now operate in a highly contestable market in which their hitherto unchallenged role in the intermediation process is being eroded by the increasingly important role of the capital markets. In the face of these structural changes, banks are under immense pressure to deliver shareholder value. The exponential growth of the derivatives markets, in particular, has created an arena within which strains imposed on banks' internal control systems bear directly on the good governance of banks.[1] More generally, the traditional ethos of banking is changing as the trading culture is absorbed more and more into mainstream banking. These changes, in aggregate, are so fundamental and far-reaching as to constitute a new paradigm.

In these circumstances, individual banks have invested heavily in developing internal control systems both to safeguard their own integrity and, also, to comply with evolving supervisory standards. In this regard, three points require discussion in some detail.

BANK CAPITAL AND INTERNAL CONTROLS

The first issue relates to the relationship between, on the one hand, capital adequacy and, on the other hand, internal controls which are in many ways a front line defence for shareholders' equity and, even more fundamentally, depositors' funds. In a sense, the Internal Control function, together with related functions such as Group Audit, have the overriding responsibility of effectively informing management's capacity to protect the bank's capital and depositors' funds. Thus, for ex-

---

[1] For a useful discussion of the relvant issues, as well as an excellent review of the recent literature, see F. X. Browne, John P. Fell and Shane Hughes, "Derivatives: Their Contribution to Markets and Supervisory Concerns", Central Bank of Ireland Quarterly Bulletin (3), Autumn 1994, pp. 37-90.

ample, the Bundesbank notes that "adequate capital banking must be the decisive security and limiting factor in dealing in derivative financial instruments."[2] In a sense, the Internal Control function, together with related functions such as Group Audit, have the overriding responsibility of informing and enhancing management's capacity to protect the bank's capital and depositors' funds. It follows that the nature, and indeed importance, of internal controls needs to be seen in the broader context of the individual bank's capitalisation set against the risks attendant in the markets in which it is operating.

EFFECTIVENESS: THE BEHAVIOURAL DIMENSION OF CONTROLS

The second issue is whether these systems are *effective* in the sense of being proof against systemic failure, fraud and/or subversion from within and without the bank. No set of controls can be regarded as immune from either a systems failure or from being circumvented or subverted. In this regard, much of the focus has, to date, been on the *technicalities* of controls — on the frequency and reliability of information, as well as on transparency of procedures and on management accountability. This is, of course, fundamental and, indeed, the IT-driven nature of banking requires such an approach.

What has, however, attracted less attention is the *behavioural* dimension of controls. In this regard, the Bundesbank has asserted that: "At the corporate level, efforts have to focus on increasing individual responsibility through improved risk-monitoring and management systems".[3] The importance of the behavioural dimension, particularly in relation to the derivatives market, stems from the fact that the line between trading and gambling is a narrow one. The aggressive trading ethos which thrives on risk-taking and is fuelled by pecuniary in-

---

[2] "The Monetary Policy Implications of the Increasing Use of Derivative Financial Instruments", Deutsche Bundesbank, Monthly Report, November 1994, p. 49.

[3] Deutsche Bundesbank, Monthly Report, op. cit.

centives, is not easily constrained within control systems predicated on traditional banking values. Senior management are, in many instances, too far removed from the realities of trading. The most robust technical systems can, for example, be subverted in the absence of systems that are informed, right from the outset, by appropriate behavioural controls.

EFFICIENCY: THE COMPLIANCE BURDEN

The third point is whether the present systems are *efficient* in terms of achieving this objective in the simplest, most transparent and equitable manner. In the UK, internal controls overseen by the Bank of England were put in place largely in response to the Johnson Matthey Bank collapse in 1984. And also, of course, in response to the growing complexity of banking and an emerging sensitivity on the part of management and shareholders — especially large institutional investors — to the importance of corporate governance. The system of internal controls varies, in some respects, between banks — depending on their size and whether, for example, they are subsidiaries of larger banks as well, of course, as on management style. But, while there are some differences in procedures and emphasis, the "core" of control systems is much the same.

These controls are, as the preceding chapters have shown, part of a much wider compliance system. Figure 8.1 on page 106 captures, in a stylised form, the scale and complexity of the compliance burden on banks.

Typically every functional unit in a bank — every cost/revenue centre — is now subject to regular audit, rigorous controls and reporting requirements by the banks' own internal capability. These are additional to prudential controls imposed by the Bank of England. Banks must also comply with statutory requirements set out in the Companies legislation and also, for example, with statutory requirements in relation to data protection. Additionally, in the UK, the Financial Reporting Review Panel monitors, *inter alia*, the presentation and treatment of financial information in banks' published accounts. More recently, banks have, in general, adopted the "best practice" guidelines set out in the Cadbury report. Those banks that provide other (non-banking) retail financial services have parallel systems of compliance procedures and controls. Increasingly, internal controls and compliance procedures are subject to scrutiny by the major rating agencies in their assessment of banks' credit standing.

In addition, external auditors report on the veracity of published financial statements (itself a major issue both for practitioners and for the authorities).[4] Post-BCCI, external auditors have a responsibility to report to the supervisory authorities any real or suspected deficiencies in financial systems, including controls.

None of these individual elements of the total supervisory regime to which banks are subject are proof against fraud or a systems failure, which is, of course, what the authorities are required to guard against. But, in aggregate, they amount to an onerous and costly body of compliance requirements.

Finally, on top of these controls, reporting accountants appointed under the 1987 Banking Act examine and report to the Bank of England on a bank's internal controls. The role of the reporting accountant is, of course, quite separate from that of, for example, the external auditor. But ultimately, all of these controls and procedures are directed towards the same end: to maintain the integrity of the institution.

The issue is whether the present arrangements — which evolved in an essentially reactive and ad hoc manner — impair the operational efficiency of an individual bank and whether a less complex, more coherent system would not provide at least the same degree of control but in a more efficient, less costly manner.

---

[4] See, for example, The Commission of Inquiry into the Expectation of the Users of Published Financial Statements (the Financial Reporting Commission), appointed by the Institute of Chartered Accountants in Ireland [Ryan Report].

Figure 8.1

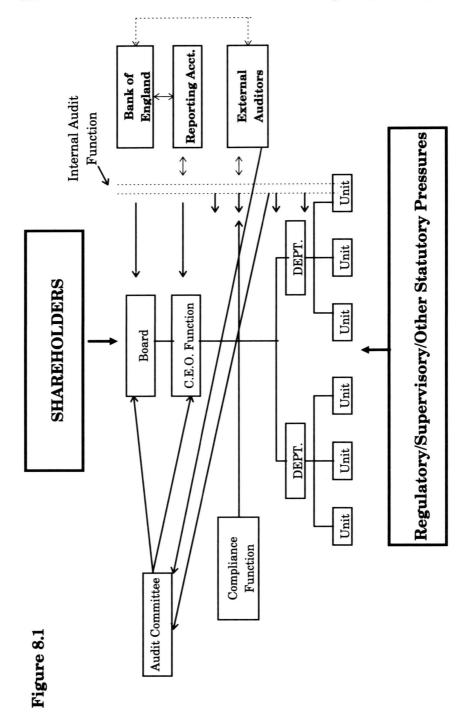

The fundamentally new paradigm within which banks now operate points to the need for robust controls which can, at the same time, be adapted to accommodate continued innovation. However, such is the pace of innovation that it is difficult for the supervisory authorities to be sufficiently informed as to manage, let alone anticipate, changes. However, failure to do so opens up the prospect of a "regulatory gap". It was, of course, just such a "gap" that, as Mogg explains, BCCI exploited. This points to the need for ongoing investment by Central Banks in enhancing their expertise (including that relating to highly advanced mathematical models used in the derivatives market) and in supervisory procedures which more effectively encompass such expertise.

It also highlights the need for structural changes in relation to, for example, clearing arrangements in the derivatives markets as well as arrangements to contain a systemic crisis in the event of a major systems failure arising from a failure, or circumvention, of controls on the part of a participant in the international payments system. And it points to the strong case for the proposed European Central Bank having a supervisory function in relation to credit institutions within the EU — an issue which was fudged in the Maastricht Treaty on monetary union.[5] In this regard, it is worth noting that the fact that internal controls are imposed at a *national* level on top of *internationally* agreed prudential and supervisory requirements has implications for the operation of credit institutions in the EU Single Banking Market. Perhaps the issue which needs to be addressed here is whether there should be a more consistent approach across countries in relation to official policy on internal controls maintained by banks and other credit institutions, or, alternatively, whether it is more appropriate that internal controls are monitored at a national level.

---

[5] This issue is discussed at some length in R. P. Kinsella, "The European Central Bank and the Emerging Regulatory Deficit" in *EMU: Transition or Re-evaluation?*, London: Lothian Foundation Press, November, 1994.

COMPLIANCE COSTS

A major issue which requires more research relates to the *costs* of the internal control function. Taken in conjunction with other statutory controls, as well as the costs of adherence to voluntary codes of conduct and guidelines, noted earlier, they represent a significant "quasi-tax". The incidence of this tax falls, ultimately, on the consumer.

From the perspective of the accountant/auditor, greater security for depositors, more robust systems and increased management accountability represent value for money for both bank shareholders and consumers. The supervisory authorities acknowledge the impact of compliance costs but argue that the ultimate cost to industry, and to the consumer, of failures arising from the *absence* of such controls would be even greater. In general, most banks would assert that they attach the highest priority to ensuring the integrity of their operations and that their internal control systems are, in fact, adequate for that purpose. The evidence is, of course, that at least some fall from grace and it is this that creates a need for intervention by the authorities. What needs to be considered is whether compliance costs could be reduced by reducing overlapping systems and procedures, all of which are (albeit from different perspectives) geared to the same objective.

INTERNAL CONTROLS AND INNOVATION

A central question, already noted above, is whether the increased importance of the internal control function is limiting the capacity of banks to respond quickly and innovatively to competitive pressures. In effect, managing a greatly increased compliance burden has created for management a major problem: how best to balance the tension between, on the one hand, innovation — which drives performance — and, on the other hand, a "control culture" which, in the nature of things, will tend to enforce a risk-averse management strategy. The growth of the internal control and compliance function, within the wider framework of prudential controls, has in effect shifted the operational centre of gravity within banks. The issue is whether it has shifted it too far and, in so doing, circumscribed managerial judgement on these issues.

In this regard, disclosure in annual reports of internal control systems is a powerful mechanism for facilitating convergence towards "best practice".[6] Disclosure facilitates a progressive strengthening of the internal control framework. Within this framework there are a number of procedures, identified in preceding chapters, which need to be highlighted. Firstly, there is the importance of ensuring that internal audit reports on controls in functional units within a bank are available as a matter of course not just to management, with whom responsibility rests, but also external auditors. The latter have, as noted, a statutory responsibility to report deficiencies to the supervisory authorities. Clearly, there is a role for Internal Audit in prioritising those particular reports which they consider to be important but the availability of all reports for review by the external auditors is an additional and important safeguard. However, the operational efficiency of even the most robust systems can be undermined by organisational fragmentation of those functions which impact one way or another on the total internal control system with a bank: Group Audit, ALCO, Credit Control and, of course, primarily the Internal Audit and Compliance functions. There is a compelling case for a simple transparent and, above all, integrated structure to ensure that deficiencies, once identified, are transmitted immediately to management. And that the corporate governance ethos is such that management immediately act upon such information.

THE COMPLIANCE CULTURE AND BANK PERFORMANCE

Perhaps the most fundamental issue for banks is that spelt out earlier by Brian Quinn — namely, how to inculcate within

---

[6] The relevance of disclosure from a policy perspective is highlighted in "Public Disclosure at Market and Credit Risks by Financial Intermediaries", Discussion Paper prepared by a Working Group of the Euro-currency Standing Committee of the Central Banks of the Group of Ten (G-10) Countries [The Fischer Report], B.I.S. Basle, September 1994.

a bank an ethical dimension; one which communicates itself throughout the bank and informs both strategy and working practices. There are, of course, "benchmark" principles and practices.[7] The reality is, however, that internal controls only work satisfactorily when they are rooted in a "compliance culture" which is, in itself, largely a product of an innate corporate sense of what is right and what is wrong.

It is interesting to reflect that the quality which was once taken for granted as an integral element of the practice of banking — the Bank of England's supervisory philosophy was rooted in it — is now the subject of seminars and MBA modules. In an era of latent, technology-driven risk a "compliance culture" based on a corporate "ethical code" is still the single most effective protection against fraud and the essential foundation for an effective, workable internal control function.

Against this background, it may be useful to outline some of the more important issues which need to be addressed in a dialogue on how best to develop, and adapt, the internal control functions to the new banking environment of the 1990s.

KEY CHALLENGES FOR PARTICIPANTS

Auditors/Accountants

- Developing a more complete understanding of the dynamics of innovation competition and performance in banking.

- Addressing the implications for the profession, and for client relations, of a significantly greater involvement in the supervisory process.

- Identifying how far increased reporting requirements, implied by Section 39 of the Banking Act — which are likely to

---

[7] See, for example, "Derivatives: Practise and Principles", Group of Thirty (G-30) Global Derivatives Study Group, Washington, DC, 1991. The US Federal Reserve has also issued "good practice" rules, as has the General Accounting Office (GAO). See US GAO, "Financial Derivatives: Actions Needed to Protect the Financial System", Washington, DC, May 1994.

be mirrored in the EU and the US — leave auditors vulnerable to litigation.[8]

Banks

- Examining how best to enhance senior management's understanding of the nature, and control, of risk, notably in relation to derivative instruments.

- Identifying, and disseminating, "best practice" in relation to internal controls across the industry, so as to minimise the imposition by the authorities of industry-wide controls as a response to the identification of faults in individual banks.

- Analysing the real costs (systems and people) of increased investment in internal controls and of the costs of the total compliance burden.

- Analysing the impact of these costs on the consumer.

- Examining how far control/compliance functions are displacing market-related functions as the fulcrum of management attention.

- Assessing how best to accommodate a human, or behavioural, dimension within technically robust internal control systems to reflect the changing, more competitive ethos in banking.

- Examining how far managerial fragmentation of related functions may impair the effectiveness of internal control systems.

Supervisory Authorities

- Developing, in conjunction with banks, systems and procedures — "early warning systems" — which can signal deviant trading activities both to management and the authori-

---

[8] The American Institute of Certified Public Accountants, to take one example, has highlighted the threat to the profession arising from the increasingly litigious environment in the US. See "US Professional Facing up to Self-Policing Role", *Financial Times* 29th August, 1993.

ties, and which are not easily amenable to subversion whether from within, or outside, the bank.

- Analysing the welfare effects of the present arrangements including, in particular, the impact of compliance costs on the consumer.

- Studying the impact of internal controls on efficiency and innovation in banking.

- Analysing how far banks' own internal controls complement or, at least in part, replicate supervisory controls.

- Examining the case for mandatory disclosure by banks of their financial and management systems for monitoring, controlling, and accounting for risk in their derivatives operations and, more generally, of publication in banks' Annual Reports of the structure of its internal controls as a means of encouraging convergence towards "best practice".

APPENDIX 1

SECTION 39 OF THE BANKING ACT, 1987

39.— (1) The Bank may by notice in writing served on an authorised institution —

    (a) require the institution to provide the Bank, at such time or times or at such intervals or in respect of such period or periods as may be specified in the notice, with such information as the Bank reasonably require for the performance of its function under this Act;

    (b) require the institution to provide the Bank with a report by an accountant or other person with relevant professional skill on, or on any aspect of, any matter about which the Bank has required or could require the institution to provide information under paragraph (a) above.

(2) The accountant or other person appointed by an institution to make any report required under subsection (1) (b) above shall be a person nominated or approved by the Bank; and the Bank may require his report to be in such form as is specified in the notice.

(3) The Bank may

    (a) by notice in writing served on an authorised institution require it to produce, within such time and at such place as may be specified in the notice, such document or documents of such description as may be so specified;

    (b) authorise an officer, servant or agent of the Bank, on producing evidence of his authority, to require any such institution to provide him forthwith with such information, or to produce to him forthwith such documents, as he may specify,

being such information or documents as the Bank may reasonably require for the performance of its functions under this Act.

(4) Where, by virtue of subsection (3) above, the Bank or any officer, servant or agent of the Bank has power to require the production of any documents from an authorised institution, the Bank or that officer, servant or agent shall have the like power to require the production of those documents from any person who

appears to be in possession of them; but where any person from whom such production is required claims a lien on documents produced by him, the production
shall be without prejudice to the lien.

(5) The power under this section to require an institution or other person to
produce any documents includes power—

  (a) If the documents are produced, take copies of them or extracts from
    them and to require that institution or person, or any other person who
    is a present or past director, controller or manager of, or is or was at
    any time employed by or acting as an employee of, the institution in
    question, to provide an explanation of any of them; and

  (b) if the documents are not produced, to require the same person who
    was required to produce them to state, to the best of his knowledge
    and belief, where they are.

(6) If it appears to the Bank to be desirable in the interests of the depositors
or potential depositors of an authorised institution to do so, it may also exercise
the powers conferred by subsections (1) and (3) above in relation to any undertaking which is or has at any relevant time been-

  (a) a parent undertaking, subsidiary undertaking or related company of
    that institution;

  (b) a subsidiary undertaking of a parent undertaking of that institution;

  (c) a parent undertaking of a subsidiary undertaking of that institution;
    or

  (d) an undertaking in the case of which a shareholder controller of that
    institution, either alone or with any associate or associates, holds 50
    per cent of the voting power at a general meeting;

or in relation to any partnership of which that institution is or has at any relevant
time been a member.

(7) if it appears to the Bank to be desirable to do so in the interests of the
depositors or potential depositors of an authorised institution which is a partnership ('the authorised partnership'), it may also exercise the powers conferred by
subsections (1) and (3) above in relation to-

  (a) any other partnership having a member in common with the
    authorised partnership;

  (b) any undertaking which is or has at any time been a member of the
    authorised partnership;

(c) any undertaking in the case of which the partners in the authorised partnership, either alone or with any associate or associates, hold 20 per cent or more of the shares or are entitled to exercise, or control the exercise of, more than 50 per cent of the voting power at a general meeting; or

(d) any subsidiary undertaking or parent undertaking of any such undertaking as is mentioned in paragraph (b) or (c) above or any parent undertaking of any such subsidiary undertaking.

(7A) in subsections (6) and (7) above 'share' has the same meaning as in Part VII of the Companies Act 1985 or Part VIII the Companies (Northern Ireland) Order 1986.

(8) The foregoing provisions of this section shall apply to a former authorised institution as they apply to an authorised institution.

(9) The bank may by notice in writing served on any person who is or is to be a director, controller or manager of an authorised institution require him to provide the Bank, within such time as may be specified in the notice, with such information or documents as the Bank may reasonably require for determining whether he is a fit and proper person to hold the particular position which he holds or is to hold.

(10) The Bank may exercise the powers conferred by subsections (1) and (3) above in relation to any person who is a significant shareholder of an authorised institution within the meaning of section 37 above if the Bank considers that the exercise of those powers is desirable in the interests of the depositors or potential depositors of that institution.

(11) Any person who without any reasonable excuse fails to comply with a requirement imposed on him under this section shall be guilty of a offence and liable on summary conviction to imprisonment for a term not exceeding six months or to a fine not exceeding the fifth level on the standard scale or to both.

(12) A statement made by a person in compliance with a requirement imposed by virtue of this section may be used in evidence against him.

(13) Nothing in this section shall compel the production by a barrister, advocate or solicitor of a document containing a privileged communication made by him or to him in that capacity.

APPENDIX 2

Extracts from
STATEMENTS OF PRINCIPLES
BANKING ACT 1987
THE BANKING COORDINATION (SECOND
(COUNCIL DIRECTIVE) REGULATIONS 1992

BANKING ACT 1987: Section 16

1 Introduction

1.1 This statement applies generally to all institutions authorised by the Bank under the Banking Act 1987 ('the Act').[1] In a number of instances however different provisions of the Act apply to institutions which are not credit institutions incorporated under the law of the UK (see specific references). The statement is made pursuant to section 16 of the Banking Act which requires the Bank to publish a statement of the principles in accordance with which it is acting or proposing to act—

'(a) in interpreting the criteria specified in Schedule 3 to this Act and the grounds for revocation specified in section 11...; and

(b) in exercising its power to grant, revoke or restrict an authorisation.'

---

[1] As amended by The Banking Coordination (Second Council Directive) Regulations 1992.

1.2 These principles are, however, not only relevant to the Bank's decisions on whether to authorise an institution or revoke or restrict an authorisation. The Bank's interpretation of the Schedule 3 criteria and of the section 11 grounds for revocation, together with the principles underlying the exercise of its powers to grant, revoke or restrict authorisation encapsulate the main standards and considerations to which the Bank has regard in conducting its supervision of all authorised institutions. The functions of banking supervision therefore include monitoring the compliance of authorised institutions with these standards and identifying any threats to the interests of depositors and potential depositors. If there are concerns, the Bank will consider what action should be taken to ensure compliance with these standards and to protect depositors and potential depositors. Where appropriate it will seek remedial action by persuasion and encouragement. However, if its legal powers are exercisable and the Bank judges that it is necessary to exercise them in order to ensure compliance with the standards or to protect the interests of depositors and potential depositors it will move to revoke or restrict authorisation.

1.3 The Act requires institutions and their officers and controllers to meet high standards in terms of their conduct. The maintenance of those standards benefits not only depositors and potential depositors but also the interests of the institution's other customers. Nevertheless the Bank's powers under the Act focus primarily on the interests of depositors.

1.4 The statement includes references to various papers published by the Bank which set out its detailed approach to a number of matters relevant to the principles, and the principles should be interpreted accordingly. Copies are available from the Banking Supervision Division, Bank of England, Threadneedle Street, London EC2R 8AH (telephone number 071- 6015082)[2]

1.5 Part 2 of that statement considers the interpretation of each of the minimum authorisation criteria in Schedule 3. Part 3 considers some issues which relate only to authorised institutions which are discount houses. Part 4 sets out the considerations relevant to the Bank's exercise of its discretion to grant authorisa-

tion. It includes some paragraphs on the authorisation of overseas institutions. Part 5 considers the interpretation of the various grounds for revocation in section 11 of the Act. Part 6 sets out the principles underlying the exercise of the Bank's discretion to revoke or restrict an authorisation.

2 Schedule 3: minimum criteria for authorisation

2.1 Before an institution may be granted authorisation the Bank has to be satisfied that all the criteria in Schedule 3 to the Act are fulfilled with respect to it. This part of the statement sets out the Bank's interpretation of these criteria. It considers first the prudent conduct criterion in paragraph 4 of the Schedule as this sets the standards of most obvious relevance to the interests of depositors, actual and potential, and to assessing whether an institution's directors, controllers and managers are fit and proper persons to hold their positions. It then considers the other criteria in Schedule 3, concluding with the fit and proper person criterion.

2.2 Where the applicant institution is a foreign bank whose principal place of business is outside the UK, in assessing whether or not certain of the criteria are met by the institution the Bank has in certain circumstances a discretion to rely on assurances from the supervisor of the institution in that place that the supervisor is satisfied with respect to the prudential management and overall financial soundness of the institution (see Part 4 below).

---

[2] The Bank's policy notices are intended to inform authorised institutions of the approach it generally adopts in relation to particular supervisory issues. The Bank's application of a particular policy in an individual case will, however, need to take into account all the facts of the particular situation and should therefore be interpreted accordingly.

Schedule 3, paragraph 4: requirement for a bank to conduct its business in a prudent manner.

General

2.3 Paragraph 4(1) of the Schedule requires an institution to conduct its business in a prudent manner.

2.4 Sub-paragraphs (2)-(8) specify various detailed requirements, *each* of which must be fulfilled before an institution may be regarded as conducting its business in a prudent manner in terms of paragraph 4(1). But, as sub-paragraph (9) makes clear, this list of detailed requirements is not exhaustive. There are other considerations relevant to whether the business is being conducted prudently. These considerations, which are sometimes summarised under the heading of the 'general prudent conduct' requirement, are described in more detail below (paragraph 2.31).

Schedule 3, paragraph 4(2) and 4(3): requirement for a bank to have adequate capital.

2.5 The Bank's general approach to the assessment of capital adequacy is set out in the following papers[3]—

Title	Date of issue
Implementation in the United Kingdom	December 1990

of the directive on the own funds of credit institutions[4] (BSD/1990/2)

Implementation in the United Kingdom of the solvency ratio directive[5] (BSD/1990/3)	December 1990

These papers were amended by the following:

Implementation in the United Kingdom of the directive on the own funds of credit institutions (BSD/1992/1)	January 1992
Verifications of interim profits in the context of the Own Funds Directive (BSD/1992/5)	August 1992
Amendment to the Bank's notice Implementation in the United Kingdom of the solvency ratio directive	November 1992

The adoption of the method of assessing capital adequacy set out in these papers implements the two EC banking directives which provide agreed minimum standards for the capital adequacy of banks throughout the EC and mirror the Basle Accord, *International Convergence of Capital Measurement and Capital Standards* agreed in 1988 by member countries of the Basle Committee on Banking Supervision[6] including the

---

[3] This approach does not however extend to the discount houses, which are authorised under the Banking Act and are supervised not by the Bank's Banking Supervision Division but its Wholesale Markets Supervision Division (see Part 3 below).

---

[4] 89/647/EEC
[5] 89/299/EEC.

[6] Members of the G10 and Luxembourg.

UK. The Bank applies this method to assess the capital adequacy of all banks incorporated in the UK.

2.6 A number of other papers are also relevant to this subject—

Title	Date of issue
Foreign currency exposure	April 1981
Foreign currency options	April 1984
Note issuance facilities /revolving underwriting facilities (BSD/1985/2)	April 1985
Large exposures in relation to mergers and acquisitions(BSD/l986/l)	February 1986
Subordinated loan capital (BSD/1986/2)	March 1986
Large exposures (BSD/1987/1)[7]	September 1987
Large underwriting exposures (BSD/l987/1.1)	February 1988
Loan transfers and securitisation (BSD/l989/1)[8]	February 1989
Implementation in the United Kingdom of the Directive on the Consolidated Supervision of Credit Institutions (BSD/1993/1)	February 1993
Country debt provisioning matrix	February 1993

2.7 Capital is defined for the purposes of paragraph 4(2) as own funds[9] (as laid down in the Own Funds Directive) and consists of Tier 1 and Tier 2 items. These are defined in the Bank's notice *Implementation in the United Kingdom of the directive on own funds of credit institutions*, as are the limits on how much certain items of Tier 2 capital may contribute to the total of own funds for supervisory purposes. Certain asset items, such as goodwill, are deducted in calculating own funds.

2.8 In order for capital to be sufficient for the purposes of the subparagraph it must be of an amount which is commensurate with the nature and scale of the institution's operations; and of an amount and nature sufficient to safeguard the interests of its depositors and potential depositors, having regard to the factors mentioned in paragraph 4(3) and to any other factors which appear to the Bank to be relevant. Paragraph 4(3)(a) refers to the nature and scale of the institution's operations; and paragraph 4(3)(b) to the risks inherent in those operations and in the operations of any other undertaking[10] in the same group in so far as they

---

[7] As amended by two subsequent notices, BSD/1990/1 and BSD/1992/2.

[8] As amended by a subsequent notice, BSD/1992/3.

[9] This definition applies in respect of UK incorporated credit institutions only. In re-

spect of other institutions the requirement is expressed in terms of net assets—that is, in relation to a body corporate, paid-up capital and reserves—together with other financial resources available to the institution of such nature and amount as are considered appropriate by the Bank. Such 'other financial resources' are in practice constituted by subordinated loan stock issued by the institutions subject to the conditions set out in the Bank's notice, BSD/1986/2.

[10] 'Body corporate' in the case of an institution which is not a UK incorporated credit institution.

are capable of affecting the institution.

2.9 In addition, in the case of UK incorporated credit institutions, in order for capital to be sufficient for the purposes of paragraph 4(3A), the institution must maintain own funds which amount to not less than ECU 5mn (or an amount of equal value denominated wholly or partly in another unit of account). However, such institutions which were authorised under the Act immediately before the commencement of the regulations implementing the Second Council Directive are required to maintain own funds of an amount not less than ECU 5mn or the highest level the institution attained at any time after 22 December 1989 (whichever is the lower).[11]

2.10 A key purpose of capital is to provide a stable resource to absorb any losses incurred by an institution, and thus protect the interests of its depositors and potential depositors. Capital must therefore have two main qualities to achieve this purpose fully—a capacity to absorb losses and permanence. All types of capital recognised by the Bank in Tier 1 have these characteristics. Tier 1 capital will not be of an appropriate nature if there are concerns that it may be paid away to the detriment of depositors' interests. Thus, for example, the Bank will only permit distributable reserves to be included in the capital base if the likelihood of

such reserves being paid away is remote.

2.11 The Bank recognises that some other types of capital also provide protection to depositors on an ongoing basis. In particular, certain other types of capital, while not meeting the two criteria of ability to absorb losses while allowing an institution to continue to trade and permanence, can provide protection to depositors. Some subordinated term debt is therefore eligible to be included in own funds subject to the conditions and limits set out in the paper *Implementation in the United Kingdom of the directive on the own funds of credit institutions* (as amended). It is an essential feature of such capital that it must be fully subordinated to the interests of depositors to give them a measure of protection against loss in a liquidation.

2.12 The Bank would not expect any element of capital regarded as permanent to be repaid except as part of a capital reconstruction it had approved. The Bank would normally only give its consent to the early repayment of capital where it was being replaced by capital of higher quality (for example, replacing term subordinated debt with perpetual debt or equity) or where the institution's need for capital was reduced for the foreseeable future.

2.13 Central to the Bank's approach to the assessment of capital adequacy is the framework of measurement set out in the paper *Implementation in the United Kingdom of the solvency ratio directive* (as amended). The

---

[11] Where there has been a change in the parent controller of the institution after 1 January 1993 the requirement is generally ECU 5mn.

measurement framework focuses primarily on the credit risk to which a bank is subject, ie the risk of counterparty default whether arising from on-balance-sheet or off-balance-sheet business. The Solvency Ratio Directive imposes a minimum standard for risk asset ratios for bank groups of 8%. (Similarly the Basle Accord established a minimum standard for the capital ratio of internationally active banks of 8%.) Although the Solvency Ratio Directive generally applies only on a consolidated basis, the Bank continues to require all UK incorporated banks to maintain a minimum risk asset ratio on a solo basis as well.

2.14 However there are other factors which are not directly addressed within this framework which the Bank takes into account in the assessment of the capital adequacy of an authorised institution. This is achieved in part by requiring institutions to hold capital against certain additional items not specified in the Solvency Ratio Directive; and in part by varying the minimum risk asset ratio applied (known as the 'trigger' ratio). The Bank sets trigger ratios for individual banks according to an overall assessment of the risks that they face and the quality of their risk management. A bank is required to meet its trigger ratio at all times. In order to lessen the risk that the trigger ratio might be breached, the Bank generally expects each institution to conduct its business so as to maintain a higher ratio (the 'target' ratio).

2.15 Part of the risk assessment for capital adequacy assessment purposes is an analysis of the quality of the loan book, for example of its concentration with regard to particular economic sectors or counterparties or geographical concentration. In order to enable the Bank to monitor concentrated positions vis-à-vis individual counterparties or groups of connected counterparties there are special reporting requirements for large exposures.[12] But other risks too are taken into account in this assessment. These include, for example, the market risks which a bank faces, in particular foreign exchange and interest rate risk, and how those risks are managed. The operational risks to which an institution is exposed, that is risks arising from negligence or incompetence in the management of either the institution's own assets and exposures or those of third parties, are covered. Risks arising from holding companies, subsidiaries, associates and other connected companies which might expose an institution to direct financial costs or general loss of confidence by association (contagion risk) are also taken into account.

2.16 The judgment formed about the risks and the institution's ability to manage those risks is largely qualitative, based on the Bank's contact with management and information provided as part of the regular returns or on an ad hoc basis. Factors

---

[12] From 1 January 1994 this area will also be covered by the EC directive on the monitoring and control of large exposures of credit institutions.

taken into account by the Bank in assessing an institution's risk management capabilities include the expertise, experience and track record of its management, its internal control systems and accounting systems.

2.17 The magnitude of foreign exchange position risk is assessed quantitatively on the basis of a formal measurement system set out in *Foreign currency exposure* (April 1981) and *Foreign currency options* (April 1984).

2.18 In the case of UK incorporated banks, risk analysis is undertaken both on a consolidated basis, in order to capture exposures arising in subsidiaries and other connected companies, as well as in the authorised institution, and on an unconsolidated basis, in order to assess whether there is an appropriate distribution of capital within a group. The second EC Directive on the supervision of credit institutions on a consolidated basis was implemented in 1993 by the Bank's notice *Implementation in the United Kingdom of the Directive on the Consolidated Supervision of Credit Institutions* (BSD/1993/1). This requires that consolidated supervision covers capital adequacy and large exposures, and extends to banks' parents and the financial subsidiaries of parents where the majority of the group's activities are financial in nature. For the purposes of the consolidated supervision of capital adequacy, the assets of financial companies in the group are risk weighted and added to the total of risk weighted assets, while their capital liabilities may be included in

own funds, provided they meet the conditions set out in the Bank's relevant notices. (Group companies which are principally exposed to market risk are subject to a slightly different treatment, which is described in the Bank's Notice BSD/1993/1.) For the purpose of large exposures monitoring, the exposures incurred by the group companies are aggregated with those of the authorised institution and measured against group capital.

2.19 Consolidated returns covering capital adequacy and large exposures form only one source of information for the Bank's consolidated supervision, which aims to form a qualitative judgment of the strength of the overall group to which a bank belongs in order to evaluate the potential impact of the other group companies on the bank. Thus, for example, where a banking group fails to meet the trigger risk asset ratio set for it, the Bank would consider that this posed a threat to the bank so requiring it to consider whether to take action in respect of the institution.

Schedule 3, paragraphs 4(4) and 4(5): requirement for a bank to have adequate liquidity[13]

2.20 An institution's ability to meet its obligations when they fall due depends upon a number of factors. In normal circumstances it depends, in particular, on the institution's ability to renew or replace its deposits and other funding, the extent to which the

---

[13] See footnote 3.

profile of future cash flows from maturing assets matches that of its maturing liabilities, and the amount of high quality liquid assets which it has readily available. Many of the factors relating to the assessment of capital adequacy are also relevant to judging the adequacy of liquidity, notably the quality of management of the institution, its internal control systems, the nature of its activities and its position in the market. Each institution is assessed in the light of its own particular circumstances, including any potential liquidity problems which could arise in group or other connected companies or other developments in or affecting those companies which could have implications for the liquidity of the institution.

2.21 Each institution is expected to formulate a statement of its liquidity management policy, taking into account the factors described above. It must identify any particular strengths and weaknesses and analyse its capacity to survive a crisis. This policy is the basis for discussions with the Bank, with the objective of agreeing minimum standards for that institution's liquidity. As part of its liquidity monitoring framework established with each institution, the institution will normally be required to comply with guidelines on the liquidity mismatches it may run in the sight-to-eight-day and sight-to-one-month bands of a maturity 'ladder' comparing its assets to liabilities and other commitments. This may be supplemented where appropriate by a requirement to hold a certain quantity of highly liquid assets.

2.22 The Bank's approach is described in greater detail in its paper *Measurement of Liquidity*, issued in July 1982.

Schedule 3, paragraph 4(6): requirement for a bank to have adequate provisions

2.23 This mirrors the Companies Act 1985 (as amended) requirement that provision should be made for depreciation or diminution in the value of an institution's assets, for liabilities which will or are expected to fall to be discharged and for any losses which it will or expects to incur. Thus provisions need to be made for, inter alia, bad and doubtful debts, expected losses on contingent liabilities (for example, connected with guarantees or other off-balance-sheet exposures) and tax liabilities. The Bank regards the accurate valuation of assets and the establishment of provisions of fundamental importance. The Bank would expect liabilities and losses (including contingent losses) to be recognised in accordance with accepted accounting standards (as embodied in the Statements of Standard Accounting Practice and Financial Reporting Standards).

2.24 In assessing the adequacy of an institution's provisions, the Bank has regard to its provisioning policy, including the methods and systems for monitoring the recoverability of loans (for example, the monitoring of the financial health of counterparties, their future prospects, the prospects of the markets and geographical areas in which they operate, arrears patterns and credit scoring techniques), the frequency with which provisions are reviewed, the policy and practices for the taking and valuation of security and the extent to which valuation exceeds the balance-sheet value of the secured loans. In some cases, clear objective indicators will be available to assist in the determination of the appropriate level of provisions; in others, more subjective judgments will need to be made. The Bank considers that it is essential that provisions be reviewed regularly.

2.25 The Bank considers that an adequate level of provisions against country debt should be made. In February 1993 the Bank issued a paper setting out a revised framework for determining the level of such provisions, which institutions could use in establishing an adequate level of provisions against country debt.

Schedule 3, paragraphs 4(7) and (8): requirement for a bank to maintain adequate accounting and other records and adequate systems of control of it business and records

2.26 The nature and scope of the records and systems which an institution should maintain should be commensurate with its needs and particular circumstances, so that its business can be conducted prudently. In judging whether an institution's records and systems are adequate the Bank has regard to its size, to the nature of its business, to the manner in which the business is structured, organised and managed, and to the

nature, volume and complexity of its transactions. The requirement applies to all aspects of an institution's business, whether on or off balance sheet, and whether undertaken as a principal or as an agent. The Bank's detailed interpretation of the paragraph 4(7) requirement is set out in the *Guidance notes on accounting and other records and internal control systems and reporting accountants' reports thereon* (BSD/1987/2 and BSD/1992/4), issued in September 1987 and July 1992 respectively.

2.27 Paragraph 4(8) of the Schedule provides, inter alia, that an institution's records and systems shall not be regarded as adequate unless they are such as to enable the business of the institution to be prudently managed and the institution to comply with the duties imposed on it by or under the Act. In other words, the records and systems must be such that the institution is able to fulfil the various other elements of the prudent conduct criterion (including appropriate systems to combat money laundering), and to identify other threats to the interests of depositors and potential depositors. They should also be sufficient to enable the institution to comply with the notification requirements which apply to it under the Act (for example, sections 36 and 38) and with requirements for the provision of information and documents under section 39 and section 41. Thus delays in providing information, or inaccuracies in the information provided, will call into question the fulfilment of the requirement in the sub-paragraph.

2.28 In assessing the adequacy of an institution's records and systems the Bank takes into account the complexity of the branch structure of the institution, and the nature of the institution's overseas operations. Owing to the difficulties of controlling overseas operations the Bank requires all UK incorporated institutions to notify it before establishing such operations. In such cases the Bank will need to be satisfied that, inter alia, the institution's systems and controls are adequate to ensure the prudent management of its overseas operations. UK incorporated credit institutions which propose to establish a branch in another EC member State in order to carry on activities listed in Schedule 1 of the Regulations[14] are required under those Regulations to give prior notice to the Bank. Under the Regulations the Bank has power to prevent a UK institution from opening such a branch in another EC member State if, having regard to the activities proposed to be carried on, it doubts the adequacy of the administrative structure or the financial situation of the institution.

2.29 Where an authorised institution proposes to establish another operation either in the UK or overseas, the Bank will require the authorised institution to have adequate internal control mechanisms for the production of any data and information which may be relevant for the purposes of supervision on a consolidated basis. This is in accordance with the Bank's notice on the *Imple-*

---

[14] The Banking Co-ordination (Second Council Directive) Regulations 1992.

mentation in the United Kingdom of the directive on the Consolidated Supervision of Credit Institutions.

2.30 Paragraph 4(8) also provides that the Bank, in determining whether an institution's systems are adequate, 'shall have regard to the functions and responsibilities in respect of them of any such directors of the institution as are mentioned in paragraph 3 above'. The Bank interprets this provision as referring to the role of non-executive directors of authorised institutions acting in a control capacity. (This is also discussed below in the context of the requirement relating to non-executive directors in paragraph 3 of Schedule 3.)

Schedule 3, paragraph, 4(9): the 'general prudent conduct' requirement

2.31 As noted above, the list of specific points in Schedule 3 relevant to prudent conduct is not exhaustive. Examples of other relevant considerations include the institution's management arrangements (such as those for the overall control and direction by the board of directors); the institution's general strategy and objectives; planning arrangements; policies on accounting, lending and other exposures, and bad debt and tax provisions; policies and practices on the taking and valuation of security, on the monitoring of arrears, on following up debtors in arrears, and interest rate matching; and recruitment arrangements and training to ensure that the institution has adequate numbers of experienced and skilled staff in order to carry out its various activities in a prudent manner.

Schedule 3, paragraph 2: requirement for the business of a bank to be effectively directed by at least two individuals

2.32 This criterion—sometimes known as the 'four eyes' requirement—provides that at least two individuals must effectively direct the business of the institution[15] In the case of a body corporate, the Bank normally expects that the individuals concerned will be either executive directors or persons granted executive powers by, and reporting immediately to, the board; and, in the case of a partnership, the Bank will look for at least two general or active partners.

2.33 Paragraph 2 requires at least two independent minds to be applied to both the formulation and implementation of the policies of the institution. Where there are just two individuals involved the Bank does not regard it as sufficient for one of them to make some, albeit significant, decisions relating only to a few aspects of the business—each must play a

part in the decision-making process on all significant decisions. Both must demonstrate the qualities and application to influence strategy, day-to-day policy and their implementation. This does not require their day to day involvement in the execution and implementation of policy. It does however require involvement in strategy and general direction, as well as a knowledge of, and influence on, the way in which strategy is being implemented through day to day policy. Where there are more than two individuals directing the business, the Bank does not regard it as necessary for all of these individuals to be involved in all decisions relating to the determination of strategy and general direction. However at least two individuals must be involved in all such decisions. Both individuals' judgments must be engaged in order that major errors leading to difficulties for the institution are less likely to occur. Similarly, each individual must have sufficient experience and knowledge of the business and the necessary personal qualities to detect and resist any imprudence, dishonesty or other irregularities by the other individual. Where a single individual, whether a chief executive, managing director or otherwise, is particularly dominant in an authorised institution this will raise doubts about the fulfilment of the criterion.

Schedule 3, paragraph 3: composition of board of directors

2.34 This provides that, in the case of an institution incorporated in the United Kingdom, the directors in-

---

[15] This requirement relates to the institution as a whole. Thus, in the case of an overseas incorporated authorised institution the Bank assesses whether at least two individuals effectively direct the business of the institution (and not just the business of its branch in the United Kingdom). The Bank would also take into account the manner in which management decisions are taken in the UK branch in assessing whether the institution fulfilled the criterion relating to the adequacy of its systems and controls set out in paragraph 4(7) of Schedule 3.

clude such number (if any) of non-executive directors as the Bank considers appropriate having regard to the circumstances of the institution and the nature and scale of its operations.

2.35 The Bank considers that non-executive directors can play a valuable role in bringing an outsider's independent perspective to the running of the business and in questioning the approach of the executive directors and other management[16] The Bank sees non-executive directors as having, in particular, an important role as members of an institution's audit committee or in performing the role which such a committee would otherwise perform.

2.36 The Bank recognises that some small authorised institutions may find it difficult to appoint sufficient suitable non-executive directors for an audit committee to be established. The Bank is nevertheless committed to the principle that UK-incorporated institutions and UK-based banking groups should have an audit committee and that, unless there are sound reasons to the contrary, all authorised institutions should appoint at least one non-executive director to undertake some audit committee functions. The Bank may consider it unnecessary for an authorised institution to have non-executive directors or an audit committee, if, for example, there is an audit committee of non-executive directors of the institution's holding company which under-

---

[16] See also paragraph 2.30 above concerning the role of non-executive directors.

takes the functions of an audit committee in respect of the authorised institution itself. (The Bank has expressed its views on the role of audit committee and non-executive directors in the consultative paper on the *Role of audit committees in banks* issued in January 1987, and in the Bank's report under the Banking Act for 1987/88.)

Schedule 3, paragraph 5: requirement for the business of a bank to be carried on with integrity and skill

2.37 This criterion is, like the prudent conduct criterion, concerned with the manner in which the business of the institution is carried on (which will partly determine its exposure to 'reputational risk') and is distinct from the question of whether its directors, controllers and managers are fit and proper persons. It covers two elements: whether the institution's business is carried on with integrity; and whether it is carried on with the professional skills appropriate to the nature and scale of the activities of the institution concerned.

2.38 The integrity element of the criterion requires the institution to observe high ethical standards in carrying on its business. Criminal offences or other breaches of statute will obviously call into question the fulfilment of this criterion. Particularly relevant are contraventions of any provision made by or under enactments designed to protect members of the public against financial loss due to dishonesty, incompetence or malpractice. (Examples of such enactments are the Theft Acts of 1968 and 1978, the Consumer Credit Act 1974, the Companies Act 1985 (as amended), the Company Securities (Insider Dealing) Act 1985, the Financial Services Act 1986, the Banking Acts of 1979 and 1987 and foreign legislation dealing with similar matters.) Doubts may also be raised if the institution fails to comply with recognised ethical standards of conduct such as those embodied in various codes of conduct. (Examples of such codes would be the London Code of Conduct for the wholesale markets in sterling, foreign exchange and bullion, the guidance notes on money laundering,[17] the Code of Banking Practice, and the Take-over Code.) As with breaches of statutes, the Bank would have regard to the seriousness of the breach of the Code, to whether the breach was deliberate or an unintentional and unusual occurrence, and to its relevance to the fulfilment of the Schedule 3 criteria and otherwise to the interests of depositors and potential depositors.

2.39 Professional skills cover the general skills which bankers should have in conducting their business as bankers, for example, in relation to accounting, risk analysis, establishing and operating systems of internal controls, ensuring compliance with legal and supervisory requirements, and in the standard of the various financial services provided to customers. The level of skills required will vary according to the individual case, depending on the nature and scale of the particular institution's activities.

Schedule 3, paragraph 6: requirement for a bank to have minimum net assets or minimum initial capital

2.40 This provides that a UK incorporated credit institution must have at the time it is authorised initial capital[18] amounting to not less than ECU 5mn (or an amount of equal value determined wholly or partly in another unit of account).[19]

2.41 An institution which is not a UK incorporated credit institution must have at the time it is authorised net assets of not less than £1 million (or an amount of equivalent value denominated wholly or partly otherwise than in sterling).[20]

Schedule 3, paragraph 1: requirement for directors, controllers and managers to be fit and proper persons

General

2.42 This provides that every person who is, or is to be, a director, control-

---

[17] Issued by the Joint Money Laundering Working Group.

[18] Initial capital is defined in regulation 2 of the Regulations.

[19] Such institutions must also continue to fulfil the capital adequacy requirements set out in paragraphs 4(2) and 4(3A) of Schedule 3 (see paragraphs 2.5-2.19 above)

[20] Such institutions must also continue to fulfil the capital adequacy requirement set out in paragraph 4(2) of Schedule 3 (see paragraphs 2.5-2.19 above).

ler or manager of an authorised institution must be a fit and proper person to hold the position which he holds or is to hold.

2.43 In considering whether a person fulfils the criterion, the Bank has regard to a number of general considerations, whilst also taking account of the circumstances of the particular position held and the institution concerned.

Directors, chief executives, managing directors and managers

2.44 With regard to a person who is, or is to be, a director, chief executive, managing director or manager (as defined in section 105 of the Act), the relevant considerations include whether he has sufficient skills, knowledge, and soundness of judgment properly to undertake and fulfil his particular duties and responsibilities. The standards required of persons in these respects will vary considerably, depending on the precise position held by the person concerned. Thus a person could be fit and proper for one position but not fit and proper for a position involving different responsibilities and duties. The diligence with which he is fulfilling or is likely to fulfil those duties and responsibilities is also considered, so that the Bank can assess whether the person does or will devote sufficient time and attention to them.

2.45 The probity of the person concerned is very important: it is essential that a person with responsibility for the conduct of a deposit-taking business is of high integrity. In contrast to the other elements of the fitness and properness criterion, the level of probity required will tend to be much the same whatever position is held.

2.46 In assessing whether a person has the relevant competence, soundness of judgment and diligence, the Bank considers whether the person has had experience of similar responsibilities previously, his record in fulfilling them and, where appropriate, whether he has appropriate qualifications and training. As to his soundness of judgment, the Bank looks to, inter alia, the degree of balance, rationality and maturity demonstrated in his conduct and decision-taking.

2.47 More generally, the Bank takes into account the person's reputation and character. It considers, inter alia, whether the person has a criminal record[21]— convictions for fraud or other dishonesty are obviously relevant to probity. The Bank gives particular weight to whether the person has contravened any provision of banking, insurance, investment or other legislation designed to protect members of the public against financial loss due to dishonesty, incompetence or malpractice. (Examples of such legislation include the Theft Acts of 1968 and 1978, the Consumer Credit Act 1974, the Companies Act 1985 (as amended),

---

[21] The Bank is permitted by section 95 of the Act to have regard to certain spent convictions under the Rehabilitation of Offenders Act 1974.

the Company Securities (Insider Dealing) Act 1985, the Financial Services Act 1986, the Banking Acts of 1979 and 1987 and foreign legislation dealing with similar matters.) In addition, it considers whether the person has been involved in any business practices appearing to the Bank to be deceitful or oppressive or otherwise improper or which otherwise reflect discredit on his method of conducting business. Some of the relevant considerations here are dealt with by the legislation referred to above. However, not all are spelt out in statute. In this connection, the Bank has regard to the person's record of compliance with various non-statutory codes, such as the Takeover Code, the guidance notes on money laundering,[22] the Code of Banking Practice and London Code of Conduct for the wholesale markets in sterling, foreign exchange and bullion, in so far as they are relevant to the fulfilment of the Schedule 3 criteria and otherwise to the interests of depositors and potential depositors.

2.48 The standards required are particularly high for those persons with the main responsibility for the conduct of an institution's affairs, although they will depend in part on the nature and scale of the business concerned.

2.49 Once an institution is authorised, the Bank has continuing regard to the performance of the person in the exercise of his duties. Impru-

dence in the conduct of an institution's business, or actions which have threatened (without necessarily having damaged) the interests of depositors or potential depositors will reflect adversely on the competence and soundness of judgment of those responsible. Similarly, failure by an institution to conduct its business with integrity and professional skills will reflect adversely on the probity and/or competence and/or soundness of judgment of those responsible. This applies whether the matters of concern have arisen from the way the persons responsible have acted or from their failure to act in an appropriate manner. The Bank takes a cumulative approach in assessing the significance of such actions or omissions—that is, it may determine that a person does not fulfil the criterion on the basis of several instances of such conduct which, if taken individually, may not lead to that conclusion.

Shareholder and indirect controllers[23]

2.50 Shareholder controllers and indirect controllers (as defined in section 105 of the Act) may hold a wide variety of positions in relation to an authorised institution, and the application of the fit and proper cri-

---

[22] Issued by the Joint Money Laundering Working Group.

[23] The definitions of a shareholder controller applying to institutions under the Banking Act depend upon whether the institution is or is not a UK incorporated credit institution. The considerations the Bank takes into account in considering the fitness and properness of a controller, however, apply equally to both categories of institution.

terion must take account of this.[24] A key consideration is the likely or actual impact on the interests of depositors and potential depositors of a person holding his particular position as controller. This is viewed in the context of the circumstances of the individual case, and of the particular position held. The general presumption is that the greater the influence on the authorised institution the higher the standard will be for the controller to fulfil the criterion. Thus, for example, higher standards will normally be required of shareholders who hold 20-33% of its shares than those shareholders who hold only 10-20%. However, in certain instances, a 10% shareholder controller would exert more influence than would normally be implied by a shareholding of this size and such a shareholder would be subject to a higher standard of assessment.

2.51   In considering the application of the criterion to shareholder controllers (and, in the case of UK incorporated credit institutions, parent controllers)[25] or persons proposing to become such controllers, the Bank has particular regard to two main factors. These are relevant whether the person is a shareholder controller

---

[24] For UK incorporated credit institutions, the thresholds of shareholding at which the fitness and properness of shareholder controllers must be assessed are 10%, 20%, 33%, 50% and 75%, together with shareholdings of less than 10% where the person is a minority shareholder, as defined in section 105(4) (a) of the Act. For other authorised institutions, the thresholds are 15%, 50% and 75%.

[25] That is a parent undertaking as defined in regulation 2 (2) of the Regulations.

or a parent controller by virtue of a shareholding in the authorised institution or by virtue of a shareholding in another institution of which the institution is a subsidiary or subsidiary undertaking.

2.52   First, it considers what influence the person has or is likely to have on the conduct of the affairs of the institution. If the person does, or is likely to, exercise a close control over the business, the Bank would look for evidence that he has soundness of judgment and relevant knowledge and skills for running an authorised institution. The Bank would look therefore for the same range of qualities and experience that it would expect of the executive directors of an authorised institution. On the other hand, if the shareholder does not, and is not likely to, influence the directors and management of the authorised institution in relation to the detailed conduct of the business, it would not be necessary to require such a level of relevant qualities and experience. In general, 10% shareholder controllers are not likely to exercise much, if any, influence or control in relation to the conduct of an authorised institution's business. Accordingly, in general the standards of competence, soundness of judgment and diligence required of such controllers will be lower than that for 20% shareholder controllers and for other controllers which hold a higher percentage of the shares of an authorised institution and to parent controllers. As regards probity, the Bank will give similar consideration to shareholder controllers as it would to managing directors, chief executives, directors or managers. The Bank also has regard in this context to whether there could be conflicts of interest arising from the influence of the shareholder on the authorised institution—this could, in particular, arise from too close an association with another company, the business or affairs of which could have a bearing on the institution's position.

2.53 Second, it considers whether the financial position, reputation or conduct of the parent controller or shareholder controller or prospective controller has damaged or is likely to damage the authorised institution through 'contagion' which undermines confidence in it. For example, if the holding company, or a major shareholder, or a company connected to that shareholder were to suffer financial problems it could lead to a run on the authorised institution, difficulties in obtaining deposits and other funds, or difficulties in raising new equity from other shareholders or potential shareholders. Generally, the higher the shareholding the greater the risk of 'contagion' if the shareholder encounters financial difficulties. The risk of contagion is not confined to financial weakness: publicity about illegal or unethical conduct by the holding company or another member of the group or a company connected to the institution in some other way may also damage confidence in the authorised institution.

2.54 In the case of shareholder controllers holding 10% or more of the non-voting shares[26] in an authorised institution or an institution of which it is a subsidiary institution the Bank takes into account the degree of influence they exert or may be able to exert. In general, because the shares are non-voting, these persons are not likely to exert much influence on authorised institutions and, therefore, the standard which they are required to meet is lower than for voting shareholders. However, situations may arise where non-voting shareholders can exert a material influence over the institution, whether by suasion or any other means, and these persons will be considered in the light of the nature of the influence which they are able to exert then.

2.55 The fitness and properness of minority shareholder controllers of UK incorporated credit institutions are also subject to assessment by the Bank. Minority shareholder controllers are persons who hold less than 10% of the shares and are entitled to exercise or control the exercise of less than 10% of the voting power (whether directly or indirectly) of the institution and, by virtue of their holding, are able to exercise a significant influence over the management of the institution or of the institution's parent company. The Bank's consideration of these persons will take into account the nature of the influence which they are able to exert—issues similar to those taken into account in the assessment of other categories of shareholder controller will be considered.

---

[26] Applies to shares in UK incorporated credit institutions only.

2.56 In considering the fitness and properness of indirect controllers it is also necessary to have regard to the precise position held.

2.57 In the case of an indirect controller who 'directs' or 'instructs' a shareholder controller, in terms of section 105(3)(d), similar considerations apply as those relevant to assessing the fulfilment of the criterion in relation to shareholder controllers. In other words, the standards which an indirect controller will need to satisfy are likely to be at the minimum the standards also required of the person who is indirectly controlled.

2.58 Where a person is an indirect controller by virtue of 'directing' or 'instructing' the board of an authorised institution, in terms of section 105(3)(d), the standards required will be high. The indirect controller would have to have the probity and relevant knowledge, experience, skills and diligence for running an authorised institution. The qualities required would be those which are also appropriate for the board of directors of an authorised institution.

2.59 The Bank expects both authorised institutions and the controllers themselves to inform it of any material developments which may cast doubt on the continued fitness and properness of the controllers or which otherwise indicate a possible threat to the interests of depositors and potential depositors.

INDEX